Gary Sloan's <u>Gang Life</u> is a must read for law enforcement, prosecutors, correctional officers and any student of behavioral science or criminal justice. Its gritty and often harsh reality explore not only the etiology of gangs and social deviance, but also provides law enforcement with a sorely needed supplemental to its arsenal; knowledge.

Rene Enriquez, 2009

Rene "Boxer" Enriquez is a 17 year upper-echelon former member of the Mexican Mafia and subject of a best selling book titled, <u>The Black Hand</u> by Chris Blatchford.

Rene currently educates law enforcement throughout the United States about La Eme and its infrastructure. He also provides expert testimony in both state and federal courts.

We often read about gang deaths and gang wars and view the consequences every night on the evening news. We wonder how this can happen and why anyone would join a gang. An honest, in-depth and hard-hitting look at gang subculture, written by Gang Detective Gary Sloan who has lived on the front lines for years.

<u>Gang Life</u> will answer many of the questions you have regarding the evolution of a gang member and the lifestyle they lead. More importantly, it offers solutions to addressing the ongoing problem of gangs.

Tim Burt
Orange County Register

Gary Sloan pours his heart and soul into a book everyone (from the college student to the veteran police officer) should read. <u>Gang Life</u> helps all of us understand how the gang problem in the United States evolved over the years and what we as a society should do about it now. It has been reviewed and validated as accurate and credible by gang detectives from across the country, and high level former gang members now working for law enforcement in an advisory capacity.

After the reader develops a thorough understanding of gangs, Sloan then goes on to explain the dynamics of creating a gang unit and the steps a detective takes from initial crime scene investigation all the way through sentencing; steps include response, surveying the scene, canvassing for witnesses, witness protection, confidential informants, follow-up at the station (computer checks), search and arrest warrants, collaboration with the district attorney, jury trial, polling the jury, sentencing, post-interview with the defendant, and continued contact with defendant and family.

Sloan has written a masterpiece that will be utilized by law enforcement and sociologists for years to come.

Pete Bollinger
Police sergeant

Gang Life

Copyright Pending©2009, Pete Bollinger and Steve Winston

All rights reserved. Any reproduction, transmission, in any form or by any means electronically or mechanically without written permission from either copyright owner is forbidden.

Police and Fire Publishing
1800 N. Bristol St. Ste C408
Santa Ana, Ca. 92707
e-mail: Bolly7@aol.com
www.policeandfirepublishing.com

ISBN: 978-0-9841164-0-9

Note to the reader: Concepts, principles, techniques, and opinions presented in this manual are provided as possible considerations. The application, use, or adoption of any concepts, principles, techniques, or opinions contained in this manual are at the risk of the individual or organization who makes that decision.

Gang Life

A comprehensive and inside look at today's gang member, authored by a gang detective who lives in their world each and every day.

Gang Life

Life and opportunity is offered to every individual as a two pronged fork; only the individual can decide which path to take. Parental, social and psychological factors can contribute to preference, but in the end, it is the individual's decision. We all have a choice.

Pictures always tell a story. Most of the pictures will have an explanation of the basics, but it is up to you to look deeper. The ability to see what others don't is what will take you to a deeper understanding of the complexities of the gang issues that face society

The information contained in this book is from a real gang detective; one who continues to work with gangs on the street. The stories and expertise come from direct interaction and due diligence of the truth. You will become familiar with gang folklore, traditions and purpose taking your education and expertise to the next level.

Modified low key detention

Table of Contents

1 Jerry Ortiz	Pg 13
2 Gang Overview	Pg 16
3 Origins of gangs	Pg 24
4 Criminal terms	Pg 39
5 Sociology of a gang member	Pg 43
6 Building rapport	Pg 62
7 Women and their roles in gangs	Pg 71
8 Telephonic and electronic monitoring	Pg 84
9 Gang culture; tattoos and graffiti	Pg 100
10 Gangs and drugs	Pg 126
11 Parental ignorance	Pg 150
12 Solving crime	Pg 158
13 Legislation and court procedures	Pg 166

14 The answer to destroying gangs   **Pg 175**

15 Anti-corruption legislation   **Pg 179**

16 Hand signs   **Pg 188**

17 Crime scenes   **Pg 207**

18 Forms   **Pg 219**

Often outmanned and outgunned, law enforcement holds the line against society's predators.

Dedication
This book is dedicated to my family, who supported me during the hardships of law enforcement which allowed me to become the person I am. Succeeding at the highest level could only be attained by the sacrifices made by my wife, who has experienced and endured every emotion and every pain an officer's wife feels. To my friend Tim Burt, who without his support and guidance this book would not be possible; and to the men and women, who on a daily basis without complaint or prejudice, wear a gun and badge to protect those who cannot protect themselves.

SPECIAL THANKS TO:
CHELA ORTIZ
ADAM CORDOVA (Graphic designer)
DANIEL LEICHT (Art Director)
TIM BURT (Editor, Orange County Register)

MARK LILLIENFELD
TIM BRENNAN
MICHAEL GAITAN (Los Angeles County Sheriff's Department)

Further, I dedicate this book to the memory of Deputy Jerry Ortiz and his family. Deputy Ortiz, a man honored and respected for his true dedication to law enforcement; may he watch over us from heaven.

Deputy Jerry Ortiz

Chapter one

The Death of Deputy Jerry Ortiz

On June 24th 2005 at 3:15 p.m., my life changed forever. Another day of dealing with society's misfortunes, taking yet another person to jail, subconsciously thinking throughout the shift, as we all do, is this the day I will not make it home?' I made it home, however, a brother officer did not. I answered my phone to the sound of a female crying. She was a close family friend who oddly stated, "I just need to hear your voice." As she gasped for breath she told me to turn on the television and watch the news. I did, and to my shock and horror, I watched as my friend, whom I had just spoken with earlier in the day, was being escorted into a helicopter for an emergency transport to the hospital. He had suffered a single gunshot wound to his head.

My friend, partner, and newly married man, Deputy Jerry Ortiz, was being lifted from a stretcher to the helicopter. It was heart wrenching to watch helplessly as officers and paramedics desperately performed CPR on his lifeless and unresponsive body. I tried to figure out how this possibly could have happened. Jerry was considered a superior deputy who feared no one and to him, death was not an option; he was in excellent physical shape and a medalist with the department's boxing team.

Jerry had been a Los Angeles County Deputy Sheriff for years. He was a seasoned and sharp deputy with a deep compassion for society, as well as enforcing the law. That day the city was shut down; not a single person was allowed to enter or leave the area of the murder unless they were identified. Hundreds of deputies arrived at the location, most coming on their own looking for answers. One of the finest homicide teams in the country was sent to the command post in an effort to help with the crime scene. The detectives recovered evidence and located the one or two witnesses who would actually speak to the police to help bring clarity and closure to the horrific event.

Numerous search warrants were issued, and hours later the suspect was found cowering in a bath tub just a few houses from where the incident occurred. This street predator was found hiding from the very people who would have protected any member of his family without judgment or prejudice. The very person the suspect murdered would have given his life protecting him and his family members.

A few months later formal charges were filed for the murder of a hero Deputy Jerry Ortiz. The sentence for the crime would be death to the person who was responsible; he was a self proclaimed shot caller from a neighborhood plagued by gang members, violent assaults, and narcotic distribution. At the trial, the events of June 24, 2005 were revealed.

On the day of the murder of Deputy Jerry Ortiz, the suspect was lying in wait behind the door that Jerry approached. He watched Jerry's every move, and made the decision to take Jerry's life. Although Jerry was of no immediate threat to the suspect, the sole mission of the suspect was to preserve his own life at any cost. He took aim as he pointed the gun between the small crack made by the door, the only thing separating him from Jerry. The suspect made a choice that would end up costing him his freedom, and would change the lives of the hundreds of family members, friends, acquaintances, and colleagues who loved Jerry Ortiz. The suspect fired one round directly at the head of Deputy Jerry Ortiz. Jerry felt no pain as he fell to the ground; the wound took his life instantly.

At the conclusion of the trial, the suspect, and alleged tax collector for the Mexican Mafia was found guilty of all counts, including committing murder at the direction of and in association with his gang. The sentence imposed was death.

Why did this happen? What could have prevented such a senseless, brutal, and animalistic event? Why would someone choose to take a life with no concern for consequences, with no care for how many this would affect? Why would someone play God?

Unfortunately, horrifying events similar to the death of Deputy Jerry Ortiz occur throughout the United States far too often. The gang lifestyle contributes to the ongoing battle which has plagued law enforcement and the wellbeing of communities everywhere for decades. Gang Life is an in-depth look at today's gang member, and the subcultures, sociology, and mentality associated with them. It analyzes the responsibilities and duties in which law enforcement has to directly take on every day in order to possibly make a difference and provide a safer community.

Chapter two
Gang overview

Older brothers are a huge influence on younger siblings. The "peewee" is emulating his hero.

I am a deputy sheriff and have been for almost two decades, and have worked as a gang detective since 2004. I have been involved in the investigation of hundreds of gang-related cases involving murder, violent assaults, kidnapping, robbery, witness intimidation, child molestation, drug dealing and the manufacturing of narcotics. These are the very crimes which perpetually fuel the gang-infested communities, promoting fear and imprisoning members of these cities in their own homes. At times while working in an undercover capacity, I observed first-hand the mentality of the gang lifestyle and the excuses used to justify their actions and need for existence. I have conducted thousands of interviews with gang members from a variety of locations and backgrounds; most of them spoke candidly and were able to give a truthful and eye opening account of what they do and why they do it.

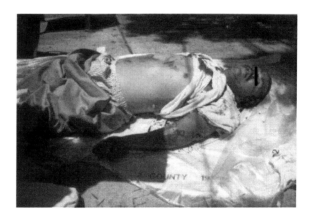

Being a gang member may look glamorous to some young people, but when the shots are fired they flee the scene and don't usually see the consequences of their choices. Only the dead and wounded are left behind for the officers and detectives to clean up.

This book is intended to assist the reader in understanding the gang lifestyle and gang members. As prevailing literature commonly does, I will not make excuses nor condone the behavior of gang members who promote fear throughout the community they prey upon. My goal is to promote knowledge and understanding of how the gang lifestyle impacts society. I wish to convey a point of view from someone who has seen first hand what the gang member views as right and wrong. This book is not only intended for a person pondering a career in law enforcement, but also for those looking for answers, or who simply desire an insight into the gang lifestyle and subculture.

Generational gang picture (notice the young male on the left)

During the course of this book, I may use incidents and stories related to the murder of law enforcement officers. This book will at no time mention the name of any suspects who took the life of any law enforcement official; their names shall in no way be honored or remembered and do not deserve any recognition as do the real heroes who have fought to protect society everyday.

Photo opportunity at a local park

Does the city have a gang problem? How much esteem does this particular gang unit carry throughout the county and state? Why do you want to be in this unit, with this department? Perhaps you have grown up in a gang area and have observed the intimidation and oppression of law abiding citizens firsthand. This would be an excellent point to bring up at some point in the gang detective interview.

Is gang affiliation a crime?
Americans have always had freedoms not enjoyed by citizens of other countries. Even when it is obvious a group of people are involved in or suspected of assembling to conduct criminal acts, they are protected by the United States Constitution. We will discuss methods officers and detectives utilize to approach the group later in the book, but the short answer is "no, gang membership or affiliation by itself is not a crime," however, it can be an enhancement when involved in illegal activity.

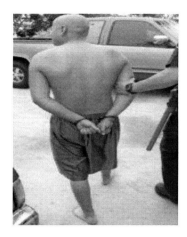

How street-wise are you? Can you tell the difference between a gang member or an individual who simply shaves his head? Is this a gang member? Why or why not? What is the definition of a street gang? Society will depend on you to protect them from gang members.

How to recognize a gang member

The average person will identify people of a certain ethnicity as gang members when in fact they are not. So how can a law abiding individual walking through a mall know? Unfortunately they can't. The look today consists of:

- **Shaved head**
- **Baggy pants**
- **Attitude**
- **Tattoos**
- **Long sleeved button up shirt**
- **With others who have the same look**

The bad boy look
There has been a trend over the last decade for individuals to appear "hard", for them to (exude) an edge. I call it the "puffy chest syndrome". The many explanations for this syndrome include, rap music, prison influence, attention from the opposite sex and the overall deterioration of society.

Many Young people today are trying to be hard, but they're not. The baggy pants, bandanas, tattoos, "gangsta rap" and a hard edge voice mail that has the individual talking like a rapper or gangster, sound ridiculous. Most of these attempts to look like a thug are laughable. Shaved head, long shorts and high socks may get you hurt, but will not place the youngster in or near the category of a police officer or detective. The polar opposite of the "hard" look, are police officers (gang detectives); generally well-groomed, short hair, wearing jeans, a t-shirt and a wind breaker type jacket marked "Police". Officers prove to gangsters on an hourly basis they don't have to look hard, to be hard. When gang members have faced fear without retreat as officers do and have actually been involved in near death situations …only then will they be hard.

Wannabes
It is sometimes difficult to determine who is and who isn't a gang member. I have stopped numerous individuals who look like a gang member and discovered they are straight A students (However, this is not always absolute. In some cultures gang members are A students). When asked why they endanger themselves by looking like a wannabe gangster they ALWAYS give the same answer, "Girls." Some of them will get **hit up** by a gang member and asked "Where you from?" The wannabe will reply "Nowhere, I go to school" or "I don't claim, I don't bang." Comments similar to these will usually appease the true gangster and result in a peaceful conclusion. Most often there will be no violence, but on occasion a truly innocent wannabe will be killed. This is tragic, but countered by officers and detectives on the street who say again and again, "If you look like a duck, walk like a duck and sound like a duck, you're probably a duck."

If you do not place yourself in harms way and do not look like a gang member, there is an almost negligible risk of becoming a crime victim resulting from gang violence. Of course, one should not provoke any situation by a statement or disapproving look.

Chapter three

Origin of gangs

How did gangs in America begin? There are over 700,000 gang members in the United States. You will hear all types of stories on the origins of gangs; let's start with some of the most well-known gangs for some insight into this very difficult question. But first understand that naming the gang is not some mysterious formula dedicated to ancestors from centuries past.

History of Gangs
Sociologists and society have painted a picture of how today's gang member looks and acts like. Limiting knowledge of the gang subculture over the last 50 years is shortsighted. Gang subculture has existed for hundreds of years. The term "thug" dates back to 1200 AD in India (thugz) referring to a gang of criminals who roamed the country pillaging towns along the way. This subculture has mutated over the years into a criminal enterprise. From the beginning, gangs were known for their reckless uninhibited persona and ideology. They took what they wanted, when they wanted and utilized fear, intimidation and membership as a basis for claiming a territory, street or city as their own. When comparing the modern day gang member to the past, we should recognize two things. First, gangs of today have shown a sophistication through technology and communication, worthy of financial gains in the billions; second, this criminal enterprise has existed within our communities for decades and has used the very same tactics of intimidation to gain these financial fortunes. The same rules governing today's gang culture were started and perfected as early as the 1800's.

Throughout American history, we have been fascinated with the gangster. Billy the kid, The James Gang and other documented gangs have categorized members of this subculture in almost a celebrity status; unfortunately, very similar to what we do today. As the 1800's took shape, there was a new generation of gang member created from the migration of those searching for a better life.

Irish gangs such as the Dead Rabbits and Jewish gangs like the Monk Eastman Gang terrorized New York City during the late 1890's. Though small in numbers these gangs used the same tactics of intimidation modern gangs do, instilling fear throughout the community. To ascertain status and claim the area's as their own these gangs created a mob of members that truly personified a new generation of murder, extortion and fear, hidden behind what they referred to as, "protection." This subculture started what would then pave the way to an even larger problem which would take hold of the citizens of these cities and one of the most notorious gangs of this era formed in the 1890's, would be the forefront of what the American people today would objectify as the "true gangster." This group, known as the Five Points Gang, because its home turf being situated in the Five Points (Bowery) Section of Lower Manhattan then outlined how gangs would operate and become financial enterprises.

The Five Points Gang was led by Italian immigrants Paola Vaccarelli, better known as Paul Kelly and his right hand man Johnny Torrio. This gang was considered one of the most significant street gangs of their time and opened up a life line between the Italian Mafia and the street gang culture. Considered the major leagues by most young street gang members, the Five Points Gang recruited its members from across New York City and was acknowledged as one step away from the Italian Mafia. Johnny Torrio, who went on to become a notorious member of the Sicilian Mafia (La Cosa Nostra) was responsible for the recruiting of younger gang members throughout New York City.

One of the most well known and prolific gang members to come from the Five Points Gang was a boy of Italian decent born from immigrant parents. This boy would rise to the top of the hierarchal rank within the Italian Mafia and would be one of the most feared and well-known gang members of this century, his name was Alphonse Capone. Al "Scar face" Capone was summoned by members of the Five Points gang after becoming a member of the James Street Gang. To maintain control of Chicago mob territories Capone became one of the most violent gangsters in Chicago and stories, books and movies to this day are still being produced about his reign of terror. Because one man could rise to the level of celebrity status and notoriety which was publicized as iconic, younger generation gang members growing up in this era emulated him. The rise of a person they identified with because of Al Capone's immigrant status and low economic foundation, created the persona of a crusader. Younger gang members dressed like him, talked like him and above all, believed in a subculture which manipulated society into believing it was necessary for protection of the city. These street gang members were influenced by mobsters, believing they could also rise to a level which in this particular era consisted of social and financial status far beyond the dreams of a person of lower income.

These younger gang members were enticed by a life style of women, fame, social acceptance from city officials and an ideology that this was a better way of life. However, just like today, gang members did not understand or recognize they were being used as pawns, patsies, and soldiers. The gang mentality took advantage of the lower class neighborhoods or "ghettos" and attempted to pass their beliefs as identifying with the lower income working citizens. Greedy officials accepting bribes and brutish intimidation of honest people in power accelerated the increase in gang involvement and their efficacy. This in turn created a divided mentality for territory. Sociological aspects played a major role and lines were divided by ethnicity, economical status and the divided mentality of the working immigrant and their children who were striving for this status and idea formed by the manipulator.

In the early part of the 20th century, gangs continued to evolve economically, but still maintained ethnic boundaries. Most gangs were made up of Italian and Irish cultures and were inclined to intimidate and influenced people of their own race. Though gangsters of European descent developed the gangster lifestyle, other ethnicities would catch up and dominate in numbers in the later half of the 20th century. By the 1940's Hispanic gangs emerged on East and West coast and a powerful gangs known as the Latin Kings and the Vice lords emerged, changing the mentality of the Hispanic gang member.

The Almighty Latin Kings and Queen Nation (ALKQN) started in Chicago, Illinois by a group gang members of Hispanic descent. The Latin Kings created an organization of "kings" ready to overcome what they perceived to be injustice against their communities. The irony of their ideology was that criminal activity by these gangs stayed within their own communities; victimizing the very people they purport to protect. Fighting a cause through education, intelligence and civil liberty did not come to fruition. The same criminal behavior by all criminal street gangs was perpetrated against their own cultures, regardless of the race or ethnicity of the gang. Violent crimes, drug distribution, extortion, and many other crimes are emulated with the same mentality as the original Italian mobster.

The Latin Kings have become the largest and most violent criminal street gang in Chicago and the original edict of purity has been eased to raise the number of members. Similar to the white outlaw motorcycle gangs the Latin Kings migrated into other states and developed chapters. These chapters were referred to as tribes and they used animal names such as, Wolf tribe and Lion tribe, etc… Each chapter had a hierarchy and was structured under the governing rules known as the King-Manifesto. By 1994, New York City authorities announced the Latin Kings as the largest and most violent criminal street gang they had ever encountered. Gangs of all races were now becoming the focal point of not only local law enforcement, but the United States Attorney's Office as well. One group in particular, had risen to national prominence in only a few decades and is considered one of the most violent criminal street gangs in the United States responsible for thousands of murders and violent assaults.

A black criminal street gang known as the "Crips" formed as a sub group in 1969 in Los Angeles. A 15 year old gang member put together a group of younger male blacks and identified themselves as "Baby Avenues." The mentality of the Baby Avenues was an emulation of an older generation criminal street gang, who had helped in the dissemination of violent acts with the notorious "Black Panthers." The Avenue Boy's, who had taken their name from living geographically on Central Avenue in Los Angeles, were fascinated with the notoriety the Black Panthers had within the criminal gang enterprise and wanted to build and develop a much larger gang. . The Cribs developed a style of dress that included an earring in the left ear and carrying a cane. They attracted local media attention after assaulting visiting tourists. The tourists described the suspects as cripples carrying canes and the paper mistakenly referred to the gang as Crips.

In early 1970, the word Crib had evolved and was accepted as Crip. This evolution of names is similar to what happened to the word, "Barrio" in the early 1980's. The letter "B" at times was pronounced in the Hispanic culture as a "V" and thus, over the decades, has even in the Hispanic culture changed from "Barrio" to "Varrio". This same evolution occurred within the Crip name within the black gangs. It had become so common for the term Crib to be pronounced Crip that it became the identifying name within the Crip ideology of criminal street gangs. Within this criminal gang known as "Crips" numerous sets surrounding the Los Angeles area became and identifying factor of the Crip gang, using it as a foundation and identifying factor for the gang they claim. They are now known worldwide and have embraced the evolution of their name. The color blue is the most obvious symbol identifying the Crips Criminal Street Gang.

This same aspect is true to the black street gang member who believes in the Crip mentality. Gangs such as Avalon Garden Crip, Eastside Crip or Inglewood Crip hold the same credence towards this identifying factor to the gang they claim, but associate themselves as "Crips".
Depending on the gang and ethnicity, traditional initiations are as different as the color of their skin and culture; a Crip prospect must commit a crime in front of a gang witness. This process called, "Loc'ing-in" which differs from the female version of acceptance referred to as being "sexed-in".

Though the Crip gang was conceived in California, it has spread throughout the United States and even to other countries. Formally known as British Honduras, a Central American Country now known as Belize discovered black criminal street gang members within the Crip ideology in the early 1990s. Crip gang members have established criminal enterprises in California, New York, New Jersey, North Carolina, Georgia, Connecticut, Florida, Pennsylvania as well as other east coast regions.

Tension regarding gang territory, ideology, disrespect and violent acts against certain Crip members, divided the black gang community in 1972. Conflict among several black Crip gang sets and non Crip claiming gang members, forced the conception of what is now known as the "Blood" black gang member. At one time, Crip sets which had expanded into non Crip territories, actually banded together and got along. One of these gangs, known as the Piru Street Boys actually hung out with members of the Crip sets and were known as Piru Street Crips. A conflict within this set with Crip gang members turned into an all out gang fight where the Piru Street Boys were outnumbered. After this conflict, members of the Piru Street Boys aligned with other gangs who also had conflict with the Crip sets, one of these conflicts ending in the murder of one of their fellow members (L.A. Brims gang member). This alliance stopped acknowledging the color blue as an identifying factor toward membership. The group of gang members adopted the opposite color red and in turn, several gangs within the Los Angeles area's who had been wronged, threatened or attacked by Crip set gang members joined what was now called "Bloods".

This "Blood" mentality did not stay in the streets of California. By 1993 the Blood Gang was known in a New York correctional facility known as GMDC (George Mochen Detention Center) as the United Blood Nation. At the time, the Latin Kings controlled most of the illegal activity within the facility and was involved in major conflict with black inmates and targeted them for attack. The black inmates who believed in the Blood set mentality developed this prison gang to combat the violence against them.

Thousands of Blood set gang members had been established across the country by 1996 and recruitment continued. Blood gang members were considered more violent than other gang members. Slashing attacks against innocent victims were common during robberies. The violent attacks were deemed forms of initiation and became a mandatory ritual for membership. This violence was not only targeting members of the community, rival Crip gang members, but against their own Blood Gang Members. In 1999, a series of meetings was attended by members of the East and West coast Bloods in an effort to align as one nation for power and unification. The meeting was successful and unified Bloods across the country who now refer to themselves as "Damu" which is a Swahili word for blood.

Gang names
How do gangs get their names? Street and city names are the most common method of naming the gang; it could also be something as simple as a television show, or initials of rhyme the founders thought was cool, or even a take-off of a local school or territory. When conducting research on the origins of a gang there will often be conflicting information with some of it based on urban legends; the name most likely evolved from a combination of factors. Truly only the founders really know.

Mexican Mafia
Comprised of Hispanic gang members from a multitude of criminal street gangs from the Southwest United States. Even though they claim a specific gang, they still identify with the rules and regulations of the Mexican Mafia.

Bloods
Originally a **faction** or **set** of the Crips gang, a set called the Pirus broke off and formed alliances with other smaller black gangs and labeled themselves the "Bloods". The color red is the most obvious symbol identifying the Blood Criminal Street Gang.

F Troop
A Hispanic gang that took its name from an old television show that was popular at the time.

18th Street
A Hispanic gang that has spread throughout the United States, originally named after a street in a large city. It has also spread internationally, with the United States recent deportation policy 18th Street Gang Members can be found in Mexico and Central America.

6th Street
However, do not assume the street name is where they congregate. For example, a gang that called itself 6th Street, loitered on 3rd Street. The founder could have originated on 6th Street, or any other number of reasons.

White Fence
An area of Los Angeles that was fenced off by the city due to complaints from passengers on a train that passed by the blighted area.

Hells Angels
A white biker gang that specializes in major narcotic transactions. This gang wears the color red and are enemies of the Vagos.

Vagos biker gang
A white biker gang that also specializes in narcotics. They wear the color green and are enemies of the Hells Angels.

Building expertise
Most gang members have stories or folklore regarding the origin of their gang; some are true, some are not. Ensure research is validated before believing one story over another or you may look foolish while rendering expert testimony. Knowledge of a gang's origin can only enhance the expertise of anyone desiring to assist society in the omnipresent gang problem.

"Experts"
An emergency room nurse argued that Bloods were a black gang and their rival Crips were a Hispanic gang. The officer tried in vain to explain the truth, but due to her encounters with gangsters in the emergency room she felt as if she were an expert. You will discover everyone is an expert and everyone grew up in a gang neighborhood. She was duped by these manipulators who no doubt had some good laughs at her expense.

Identification of gang members
There are many ways to identify a gang member and place him in the system as a gang member or associate of the gang that accepts him.

Pride
After a legal or consensual stop the gang member will brag to the officer regarding his status. Whether or not he was jumped-in, and who he would back up during an altercation.

Rapport
Officers develop relationships and a mutual respect with the gang members who often disclose the truth to an officer or detective. This is not a one-sided relationship as the officer/detective can offer protection and an "opportunity" to give up the gang lifestyle.

Arrest
After an arrest and the subject understanding he will be in-custody, the gangster will volunteer the fact he is a gang member for his own safety. Understanding being housed in a cell with a rival may be detrimental to his health.

Associates/Affiliates
Non validated gang members who can be linked directly to a particular gang; continuous contact with the police while in the company of other gang members. If the police can reasonably determine through a gang expert that the individual is connected with the gang, they will be subject to additional penalties if arrested.

Penal Code 186.22
This form is completed upon contact with a gang member, suspected gang member or associate of a gang member. This Penal Code Section articulates additional penalties for gang members or associates who commit a criminal act for the benefit of their gang. This section has been extremely effective in gaining additional penalties for violent criminals and curbing gang crime and intimidation.

Probable cause
There are two basic types of stops; probable cause and consent. Probable cause consists of many different types, for example, any traffic violation, any pedestrian violation (jaywalking etc...), any crime, however small (littering), and/or suspicious activity. Once a police officer witnesses any of these situations a detention is legal. While investigating the incident the officer can formulate other reasons during the contact (probation,

parole, warrants) to search the person detained and/or his or her vehicle. It should be noted that recent case law limits officers' ability to search a vehicle, though a resourceful police officer has never been stymied by the Supreme Court.

Consensual encounter
The second way is consent. Most contacts are consensual and experienced officers make most of their felony arrests using this tactic. It must be apparent to the district attorney that the officer had both permission to contact and permission to search the subject for them to file the case. If the officer is unclear in the report, the case will not be filed.

Officers often attempt to make a consensual contact even if they have enough probable cause as a low key approach eases the tension of the moment and plays out more like a conversation than an interrogation. However, if a subject refuses to speak with the officers the stop will quickly turn into a detention.

Reasonable suspicion
A police officer not only has a right to investigate suspicious activity he has a duty. If the officer reasonably believes **criminal activity is afoot** any detention will be legal.

Obtaining photographs
Now that you understand that simply being a gang member is not a crime, you may be curious as to how pictures are obtained which ultimately assist law enforcement in future investigations. Below are several methods of obtaining photographs.

Homicide scenes
They are usually chaotic for the initial responding officers. One or more victims are lying on the ground with gunshot or stab wounds. The people who remain in the area are dazed or emotional. There are individuals who are armed and vehicles that were blocked in and could not leave the driveway or street that have weapons in them. The responding officers

must contain and control the scene and attempt to identify each individual. At this point the officers have a right to detain anyone attempting to leave; after all a murder just occurred and they were present. A crime scene officer will begin taking pictures of the scene including individuals who will later claim they were not there. It will be up to the detectives whether or not to take photographs and fingerprints. Pictures can also link one friend to another and will assist in the conclusion of the case.

Misdemeanor crimes and photos
There must be a mutual understanding between gang detectives and gang members. When an updated photo is needed by law enforcement there are two basic methods of obtaining one; consent or arrest and the understanding by the gang member that the photograph is inevitable. The best method for all involved parties is for the gangster to agree to the photograph and to cooperate with the detective. Total honesty and cooperation will create a professional relationship resulting in a reduction in unnecessary anxiety.

The second method is to arrest the gang member for a crime. There are hundreds of misdemeanor crimes at the detective's disposal. A few of them are:

- **Drinking in public**
- **Minor in possession of alcohol**
- **Possession of narcotic paraphernalia**
- **Driving under the influence**
- **Loud music**
- **Traffic warrants**

After one of these arrests the detective can issue a citation at the scene, or transport the individual to jail. At this point the arrestee will be subjected by law to a photograph.

Photographs and criminal investigations

Photographs obtained through arrests can be placed in what is called a "**six pack**". A six pack is a random computerized collection of six photographs of the same race and characteristics to be used to identify a suspect of a crime. All six of the individuals have been arrested before and their photos are now a permanent part of the database. The detective will read an admonishment to the victim and/or witness similar to:

The person who committed the crime may or may not be one of the individuals I show you. Do you understand?
Simply point to the picture you recognize and tell me why you recognize him/her. Do you understand?

Confirmed suspect
If the suspect was identified they will be told to circle the picture and initial under it. The detective will follow up with the updated information and obtain a warrant if the suspect was clearly identified.

Injunction
Law enforcement make millions of arrests a year with a significant number being gang members. The judicial system is hot and cold with its treatment of gang members. Depending on the political climate at the time, the district attorney will decide whether or not to tackle the gang issue. The current trend is to file a gang injunction with the court; in essence filing a restraining order against each and every identified member of the gang. The injunction will prohibit loitering, being with another identified gang member, specific locations and wearing specified colors.
Many of the gangsters will challenge the order, but if dealt with promptly their challenges will wane. Some gang members will demonstrate secret defiance and resort to wearing gang colored underwear. If an officer somehow legally observes the underwear the subject can be arrested.

Gang initiations

If a passerby did not know what was actually happening it would look like a wrestling match with few punches thrown. To the expert it is an initiation into a gang; a **rite of passage** that will pledge the young persons loyalty until death. In some cases a method of gang initiations regarding females is a ritual known as **sexed up.** A woman rolls a set of dice and must have intercourse with the number of gang members in relation to the number displayed by the dice. If a female is **sexed in** she holds less respect from the gang than a woman who is jumped in. It may be difficult to a rational thinking human being why an individual would participate in this type of activity. The reasons are central to the theme of this book; acceptance, recognition and status.

Signs

Unlike the **American Sign Language (ASL)** gang signs are a form of improvised non-verbal gesticulation. **Throwing signs, hitting up, banging on** or any of the other dozen terms intended to explain digital manipulation (finger position). Children in the neighborhood learn how to contort their fingers to display letters or numbers configuring the "logo" of the local gang. An example is making the fingers look like the letter "W" signifying Westside.

An individual should never play around and utilize gang signs. It may become part of who you are and if you happen to do the wrong thing at the wrong time could endanger you and your family.

Gangs in the military

According to one high ranking military officer, the mid-90s were a tumultuous time for the American volunteer military. Gangsters were in every branch of the service and in most positions. Most of them left the rivalries with other gangs at home, but a few crossed the line. They were quickly dealt with and discharged from the service. The gang members who returned home on leave had a difficult time disregarding old loyalties and were caught up in their old world. A few were killed, but the majority of them reintegrated into the gang culture, had trouble with law enforcement and ultimately received a bad conduct discharge, dishonorable discharge and/or have served time in a jail or prison. The officer found it somewhat ironic that the gang problem significantly slowed after the 9/11 attacks; he attributed the decline to several possibilities.

1. The military has not given the infiltration of gangs the attention it should due to the war in the Middle East
2. The number of enlistments has declined, consequently reducing the number of gang members.
3. Cowardice of gang members causing a decline in enlistments.
4. New background checks policies implemented by the United States Government.

Chapter four

Criminal terms

You must begin to familiarize yourself with the significance and the meanings of tattoos. You will hear many different explanations from officers, inmates, parolees and probationers. Most of them will be inaccurate for a variety of reasons. Criminals may want to **play** with you or claim ignorance to mitigate any additional charges; Probation, Parole and Police Officers may truly believe they know the terminology, when in fact they do not. According to Retired Police Sergeant Ken Whitley, terms change as often as phone numbers. They may also have different meanings depending on geographic or cultural regions.

You must also be aware that most criminals have a need to be **hard** and impress anyone who will listen. So take what they tell you with a grain of salt and corroborate the information with other officers prior to accepting it as fact. Using the wrong slang can be embarrassing, and worse could jeopardize a case by demonstrating a lack of credibility to the gang member.

STREET SLANG

During interviews you will hear terms you may not be familiar with. Some of these terms are universal and some are tailored to a specific geographical area. It is vital to you and the community you protect that you understand their meanings.

Some of the common tattoos are:

A Tear drop………….In past "killer" now too many meanings
A star……………….Symbolization of territory
Mi Vida Loca………..My Crazy Life
Names………………..Their name, mom's, child's or wife's
Initials………………..Names, or gang affiliations
Happy face/sad face….Smile now, cry later

Some of the common terms are:

AD SEG	ADMINISTRATIVE SEGREGATION
BEEF	A CRIME
BULLET	1 YEAR PERIOD OF TIME
115	SERIOUS DISCIPLINARY REPORT
128	LESS SERIOUS CHRONO
G.P.	GENERAL PRISON POPULATION
KITE	NOTE OR LETTER
PROGRAM	HOW A PRISONER DOES HIS TIME
ROLLED UP	ARRESTED

SHU SECURITY HOUSING UNIT

SHANK PRISON MADE KNIFE

SLEEVED ARMS COVERED WITH TATTOOS

STAFF CUSTODY PERSONNEL

TATS TATTOOS

Additional vocabulary

A.B/ BRAND..................ARYAN BROTHERHOOD OR
BGF..............................BLACK GUERRILLA FAMILY
CARNAL.....................MEXICAN MAFIA MEMBER
C/O...............................CORRECTIONAL OFFICER
CHRONO......................INSTITUTIONAL WRITE-UP
CLIKA……………………HISPANIC TERM FOR SUBSET OF GANG
CRIB/PAD……………….LIVING QUARTERS
DIRTY BOTTLE.............POSITIVE URINE TEST
DORM...........................HOUSING UNIT
EME..............................MEXICAN MAFIA
GATED OUT..................RELEASED FROM PRISON
GETTING POKED……...FORCIBLE ANAL SEX
GRANDFATHERED IN..GANG MEMBERSHIP W/O BEING JUMPED IN
GREY GOOSE...............CDC BUS
GUNS............................WELL-DEVELOPED ARMS
HIT.................................A KILLING
HYPE……………………..IV DRUG USER
INK.................................TATTOOS
IRON..............................WEIGHTS
ISSUE............................CRIME
LOPP..............................INDIVIDUAL CONSIDERED DUMB

LWOP	LIFE WITHOUT PAROLE
IN THE MIX	KNOWLEDGE OF CURRENT POLITICS WITHIN THE GANG
NESTER	NUESTRA FAMILIA GANG MEMBER
N.F.	NUESTRA FAMILIA
NORTENO	NORTHERNER
ONE TIME	POLICE
PAL	PAROLEE AT LARGE
P BAY	PELICAN BAY PRISON
PECETA	PROTECTIVE CUSTODY
P.O.	PAROLE OFFICER
P.C.	PROTECTIVE CUSTODY
PECKERWOOD	WHITE BOY
PINTA	JAIL
PRUNO	PRISON ALCOHOL
PUNK	HOMOSEXUAL IN PRISON
RIPPED OFF	FORCIBLE ANAL SEX
STAFF	CUSTODY PERSONNEL
TERM	SENTENCE
TAIL	PAROLE
TIER	LEVELS OR STORIES
TIPPED UP	AFFILIATED WITH A GROUP
TOPPED OFF	OFF PAROLE
WHACKED	KILL
YARD	OUTDOOR REC AREA
YOKED	BUILT FROM LIFTING WEIGHTS
24/7	ALL DAY EVERYDAY
602	INMATE APPEAL FORM
8 TO THE GATE	1/2 OF A 16 MONTH TERM TO PAROLE
TERM	CREDIT FOR WORK TIME
5-0	LAW ENFORCEMENT PRESENCE

www.convictsandcops.com

Chapter five

The sociology of a gang member

"The truth can create contempt, however, understanding the truth is what we must live by." --*GARY SLOAN*

The three main sociological levels of a gang member are:
- Acceptance
- Recognition
- Status

According to Webster's Dictionary, the terms are defined as follows:

Acceptance:
1 agree to receive or undertake; 2. Regard favorably or with approval; 3. Believe or receive as valid or correct; 4. Take on (a responsibility or liability); 5. Tolerance or submit to.

Recognition:
1. The action of **recognizing** or the process of being recognized; 2. **Appreciation or acknowledgment**; 3. Formal acknowledgment.

Status:
1. Relative **social or professional standing**; 2. **High rank** or social standing; 3. The position of affairs at a particular time; 4. Official standing.

In all of my years as a police officer and gang detective, I have come to one conclusion as to why a gang member chooses such a heinous lifestyle. The reason for the decision to join a gang is 100% **personal choice**. Now how did I arrive at this conclusion? A gang member needs to commit acts of violence and intimidation, which is understood at the time of gang initiation and conception. Why a person decides a life filled with uncertainty, violence, rage, incarceration, and murder can truly only be answered by the individual making the poor choice. So one might ask themselves why does a person take a chance in living the "gangster lifestyle" and embrace every down fall that comes with it.

There is a saying in law enforcement that describes the gangster lifestyle. "You will end up in prison or dead." Why would anyone choose death or prison voluntarily? Why would a person chance life or death, and choose a life where there is no looking back and no hope? These are the questions that I will attempt to answer.

Regardless of the reason one chooses to take on the lifestyle of being a gang member, once that choice is made it can not be reversed. Once an individual makes the decision to join a gang, the gang owns them. A person, who is **jumped in**, or **grandfathered** in by personal choice, can not reverse their decision once they have taken the path. In thousands of interviews and interrogations with gang members, not one of them has claimed to have been forced into the gang. Not once has a gang member stated, "I was tired of getting beat up," or "I was forced to be jumped in," or "I was forced to join by my family."

In fact it was always the opposite when asked the question of why they chose a life of violence and inevitable incarceration; it was their own personal decision to join a gang. From data collected from interviews, findings and studies of today's gang member, a very high percentage say it was their sole decision to be a part of the gang; they asked for membership through whatever ritual or initiation necessary to become part of the criminal enterprise known as the **neighborhood.**

Two major characteristics exhibited by a gang member are:

Social needs

Psychological dependency

Other characteristics that fall under the categories associated with the sociology and psychology of gang members are: anti-social behavior, social, domestic, and socioeconomic status can and often do contribute to an individual's decision in giving their allegiance to a gang. Anti-social behavior is displayed through a variety of activities: disengaging from school functions, withdrawing from society and family members and not conforming to society's rules.

I have studied theories of gang involvement, but more importantly have had the opportunity to speak with thousands of gang members over my years as a law enforcement officer. Frequently the gang member had withdrawn from society in a formal social manner and filled themselves with a fantasy concept of what they believed to be acceptable. They did not view themselves or their personalities as different from the people that surrounded them, however, they did not conform to the social boundaries that society considered appropriate.

The gang member's mental framework is such that they create their own rules without moral constraints, and develop a skewed ethical outlook. The gang member lives by what they consider to be the rules, ethics, and oaths that are central to the gang. This has been corroborated through hundreds of investigations, interviews with gang members and the criminal actions in which they commit on a daily basis. Why does the gang member continue to live a life of criminal behavior, with full knowledge of what the inevitable will bring: death or imprisonment?

The answer; **acceptance, recognition, and status**.

Gang members have described in detail their actions and criminal background in my interviews and interrogations. A resounding theme seems to be once again that at no time were they ever forced into becoming a gang member; they made their own decision without listing intimidation as a factor. They truly grasp and accept what they have voluntarily entered into; a life which has proven for decades to end in imprisonment, death, or both. They accept this as their reality. The concept of why a gang member chooses this lifestyle has been theorized by professors, liberal groups, psychologists and self-proclaimed experts. For their own personal gain they have commonly used economical status to excuse gang affiliation and justification as to why a person chooses the lifestyle of gang membership. In short, they are wrong.

In turn, these theories and discussions always fail to answer the question of why gangs exist and continue to proliferate. Social environments do affect an individual's foundation and personal growth--however individuals sharing a similar socio-economical status or geographical location are not necessarily a forcing determinant for all of them to share the exact same mentality and ethics. There are countless success stories of men and women who come from broken homes, gang and drug infested areas of low income neighborhoods that have transcended their social environments, rising to the highest levels of achievement. Conversely, I have met gang members who attended the most prestigious colleges in the country, yet prefer to live the life of a gangster. This has major implications toward the popular theory of a gang member, which suggests lower economical status as a determinant for gang membership. Since many people from low income communities do flourish, and only a fraction are actually members of a gang, the socio-economic theory can not be established as credible.

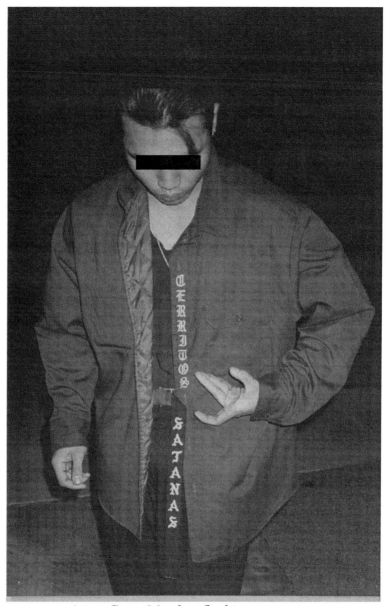
Asian Gang Member flashing gang sign.

Acceptance
I am often called upon to testify as a court-appointed expert on gangs and tasked with explaining to the judge and jury why certain crimes are gang related or committed for the benefit of, and at the direction of, or in association with the gang. In every instance my testimony as to the sociological aspect to why gang members do what they do involves the same 3 concepts: "**Acceptance, Recognition** and **Status**." The three components become the social time line in which **every gang member** will go through.

Young males and females who choose this lifestyle go through a period of acceptance. This is caused by numerous factors, and can be argued by experts who theorize this step is a form of anti social behavior; the person who is subjecting themselves to this lifestyle does not possess social skills that are acceptable by their peers. This person is at their most vulnerable point and is easily preyed upon by other gang members.

This individual is looking for self-worth. Self-esteem has been minimized by factors such as domestic violence and abuse of any kind, child molestation, and generational family members affiliated with a gang and substance abuse. They seek not only social acceptance, but an identity as to who will accept them for who they are. At times, the person is searching for someone or a group who will provide guidance and support; an entity that makes the decisions for them and alleviates the responsibility of doing it themselves. The gang lifestyle on the surface can be as intriguing as any social group or function. They are subjected to parties which present an availability of women and men on an intimate level who share the same beliefs, and possibly suffer from the same social and domestic problems. They co-exist and excuse this dangerous lifestyle and beliefs by interpreting what they see as normal human behavior. They are driven by the social awakening which overpowers them almost overnight; belonging to something bigger than themselves becomes a driving force. Immaturity and ignorance play a huge role in adapting to this lifestyle, but for most it starts off as any social atmosphere does,

seemingly harmless.
They are not immediately exposed to the violence and ugly side of gang life, in which participation will be required at a later time. They are manipulated into thinking the gangster life is similar to that of a celebrity, party all night and sleep all day. The person is accepted by higher ranking members who they may have known from the neighborhood or school earlier in life.

Another connection leading to acceptance is friendships from older siblings. These admiring relationships lead to subconscious exposure that forms an idea of role models and role model behavior. The person evolves into a manufactured product, all the while being manipulated by what is referred to as, the **older homies**. They try and emulate who they admire in various ways including how they dress, speak, and act. They also expose themselves to the social climate for acceptance, which ends up being something they can never turn away from. Ultimately they reach the point of no return and take the path which ends up culminating into the two inevitable outcomes, prison or death.

Prison

Gang members will eventually call this home.

The person has now been transformed and molded into a soldier and will be instructed to commit deviant acts to discover their true identity and purpose for the neighborhood. The person is given a moniker or a nickname, and has been educated on law enforcement detection and how to avoid arrest. The rules of the gang are explained in detail, and strongly emphasized as the primary principle that the gang takes precedence over anything, including their families.

They have entered a world which they consciously or subconsciously had yearned for; they gain **acceptance** regardless of the price or repercussions. They are asked, with no intimidation or fear, if they are willing to give their life to a group who believes in them and for the **good of the neighborhood.** They are told they need to be strong in numbers, to fight the enemy rivals and even law enforcement. They are told they will always have the backing of the gang whether in trouble, attacked by rivals or incarcerated. In turn, they must be willing to sacrifice their own life for the gang.

Gang member killed in front of his own residence laid to rest.

The person does not hold the maturity or intellect to understand the damage of accepting this lifestyle. It is difficult to comprehend the need for protection from an enemy that does not exist in their current world. Through manipulation and acceptance, the person makes the decision to become one of them. To be part of a family or friendship they have longed for, they have made the decision to **become a gangster**.

Rituals

There are many rituals a **prospect** must go through to be accepted into the gang. Different races and gangs have a variety of initiations.

Black gangs require prospects to participate in a violent crime.

Hispanic gangs require the prospect to be **jumped in.** This consists of several gang members attacking the person wanting to be accepted. The purpose is to show the person's heart and endurance, and to see if they can continue to fight, even when the person being attacked is outnumbered.

Asian gangs conduct rituals similar to that of Hispanic gangs and require prospects to be **jumped in.**

White gangs, especially white outlaw motorcycle gangs, require a pledge to become a slave to all members of the gang for a period of time in order to be a full fledged member. When the prospect has been accepted and vouched for, in decades past the prospect would lie on the ground while members defecate and urinate on them.

Regardless of the ritual or manner in which pledges are accepted to a gang, the outcome is the same: you are a gang member for life, regardless of anything, and no one can take it from you, that is, no one outside the gang. A gang member can be ridiculed by their peers for violating a code or cooperating with law enforcement and although their status can be taken as a result, the aspect and manner in which a person was made a gang member can never be taken from them. They still have the right, at any time, to claim the neighborhood into which they were accepted.

Nicknames

The gang member has now accepted their role in life, and has been made a part of something special in their eyes. They have been accepted without judgment to their physical stature or deformities, their domestic past, financial status or criminal background. In actuality the gang member is praised for their idiosyncrasies and flaws. Often named for their imperfections, like "Flaco" if the person is skinny, "Gordo" if the person is heavy, and "Mumbles" if the person has any type of speech impediment. They have been transformed and found purpose in life. This purpose however comes with a price, and this decision has branded them for life.

Recognition

Once a gang member has been accepted to a neighborhood, the lifestyle they were exposed to during the initiation and manipulation process does not change. The gang member is now introduced to more information regarding the politics of the gang; they are entrusted by other members and older so called, "**homies**" within the rank structure of the gang. The parties continue, the acceptance is overwhelming, and the newest addition to the neighborhood is captivated by their sudden fortune and fame. The newest addition to the gang family is brainwashed by the older generation gang member; this newest member is shown the ideology of the neighborhood and the rules governing this lifestyle. In the Hispanic gang culture this is referred to as La Causa (the cause). The younger gang member is introduced to this psychological metamorphosis searching for a familiar cultural group. The more experienced gang member accepts this person beginning yet another cycle of manipulation. They are asked to help in the sales and distribution of drugs, all the while being promised a "cut" of the profits. They are asked to go on small missions, commonly referred to as **puting in work,** and tested on their worthiness for bigger responsibilities.

They listen to the other gang members who were responsible for the creation of the newest member during meetings or **juntas** as they are referred to in the Hispanic gang culture. All too impressionable, the newest arrival wants to be recognized as a person who can be trusted and who can be perceived as worthy of his new position and identity in life. The new gang member wants to be recognized as someone who could be entrusted to anything the gang requires of them, regardless of the consequences it may cause to the people close to them. It makes no difference if it is family, friends, children, or strangers; they will do anything to gain the respect of their newfound peers.

The gang member desires to be recognized by the neighborhood as a **down** member, someone who will act for the benefit of the gang. The gang member watches as people of importance and rank make decisions about the gang. They want this power; they want to be seen as superior and recognized as a soldier. This feeling is overwhelming and can be addictive. The gang member will, with the help of others and a drug-induced euphoria, act in any means to perpetuate themselves toward the recognition they yearn for. How is this accomplished?

The way the gang member was manipulated into seeking acceptance is the same way that the member is fueled toward further desiring this lifestyle. They see the other gang members who have accomplished the recognition they are looking for and slip into their own role. The gang preys upon the new member's desire to achieve and soon asks him to demonstrate his or her allegiance by accomplishing what is needed and what has been set forth as true to the gang. The gang member sees this as a challenge, or a chance to prove to the gang that they have chosen correctly. It is an opportunity to further his or her rank status and become recognized as a true soldier who is willing to, without the fear of incarceration or death, subject himself to the mission at hand. The new recruit wants to show the people who had so much faith in him as a soldier that he is to be trusted. The missions can vary: act as a look out during drug sales, be a driver during a robbery, or even given the chance of true allegiance as the gun is placed in his hands to commit a crime.

Rational thinking is non-existent; the rules of society and religion do not exist. The gang member has been shown a new set of rules which are the only rules that shall apply in this world. They have been exposed to the politics within the structure, and told by the more experienced gang members that created them what is constituted as right and wrong. These rules do not change; the gang member's life is now structured with apparent meaning. The gang member has been placed in a situation of proving their true worth to a group which has asked for nothing in return until now.

The gang member has been stricken of any moralistic values, and broken down into a machine which only answers to one entity. The words spoken to them during the period of acceptance have become gospel, and the gang member is reminded daily of these words. The person is transformed into a replica of that gang, and wants the recognition they believe they deserve. They are not only tasked with "putting in work", but they take it upon themselves to act on it instinctively without provocation. They are of the mentality that at all times they are to be aware of and act upon any situation that will benefit the gang.

Gangs feed off of intimidation and fear and continually remind the community that they run the city. This can only be accomplished by the very person who has sat and waited for their turn for power. The gang member who has been recognized by their peers and the good people of the community is the person to fear. They are well-known for being the one who is willing, without malice or forethought to show their allegiance to the gang who accepted them, and be recognized as a soldier.

The process regarding the recognition timeframe for a gang member can be slow or swift; regardless, the new member knows that at some point and time, they will be recognized. Many aspects can be attributed to the quickness of a gang member's rise to the level they strive for: including generational status from siblings and parents; the amount of "work" they put in; and their level of intelligence.

I have seen gang members of high ranking status with degrees, diplomas, and even military service with medals and commendations. Some gang members have been raised in affluent areas within the community and have shown high levels of intelligence and social skills. These psychological skills eventually propel this individual to the level of what is referred to as the **shot caller**.

Regardless of social status, geographical areas in which the gang member was raised, and economical status, gang members who aim to hold the keys will aim to rise to the highest level; this wish, however, will come at a price. This price will consist of many obstacles, with incarceration being the most common. The gang member will have established themselves through violence, loyalty, and the willingness to overturn any boundaries society has proclaimed as normal. Any good hunter will tell you that most animals, once given the taste of blood, spend the rest of their lives craving it. They have been exposed to a feeling of euphoria which transposes them into a killer, not for the sake of killing, but to continually satisfy the craving which has sent them into an emotionally frenzied state of mind.

Theory of Transition

The transition from recognition within a gang, to a status and leadership role is strangely similar to a promotion in the non-gang world. The gang member has been given a taste of what they want, and they seek out what they believe to be owed to them. They have "put in their time" and proven to the gang they are a worthy soldier; recognized as someone to be feared as well as trusted.

But the euphoric feeling of recognition has passed and they are searching for more. The gang member inevitably experiences an emotionally overwhelming selfishness, which can not be reversed because they have already made their choice.

The gang member continues to work their way through the ranking structure. Politics, believe it or not, play a large role in this path. Where does the gang member come from, how much time have they done in state prison, what were they willing to do and what have they done to earn the respect of so many? Does the gang member possess the leadership skills to run a gang, a city, or a yard in prison? All of these factors play a role.

The breakdown in structure within gangs is where the rise of an individual can hurt the foundation of the gang. Imagine how many gang members within a community are looking for the same status in which they all believe to be worthy. They want a leadership position and to control the finances within the gang, to keep drug sales structured so they still get their cut, and to make the every day decisions which will affect the entire criminal enterprise. They want to make the decisions such as who is **in the hat** or should fall on the **hard candy list**. This term is for a gang member who has wronged the gang in some fashion and has been deemed as disloyal. Thus, anyone on the "hard candy list" is doomed to be eliminated.

Gang Member who was in the wrong place at the wrong time and was greeted with a shot to the head.

The political whirlwind within this decision of who is worthy to hold the keys can be an enormous task and taken very seriously by the older generation of gang members who have the power to make these decisions. The gang member who has made the choice to put themselves in the position of influence and rises to a significant level of status may now be viewed as a threat. Fellow gang members who they grew up with at a young age have possibly become their enemy during their rise in rank, commonly referred to as politicking. To be given a level of status in a gang, one must show loyalty to the gang which created them and gave them life and an identity.

They are to show no bias or prejudice towards any one member and their decisions are to be made solely for the benefit and continuous escalation of the criminal enterprise they have grown to accept as their own family. As the saying goes, "don't take it personally, it's just business." Families and children take a back seat in the priority levels of the gang member who *yearns* for a status level beyond others. The gang member who has shown unparalleled loyalty to their new family and way of life, will ultimately discover they have been manipulated and lied to. They were lied to by the same *social deviant* that created them and used as just another pawn whose importance is eventually dismissed.

Epiphany

Despite all of the factors which can contribute to one's rise in status in a gang, they will later find out everything they did was for the benefit of one person. This epiphany usually comes when the gang member finally becomes incarcerated, and is set to lose a major portion of their life for their gang. They realize that it was all done for the same person they aspired to be, the same person they looked up to for guidance and the answers to the problems they believe society had bestowed upon them. All along the problems were simply a manifestation the gang member created through the choices they had made and the thoughts that had been programmed into them. The gang member finds out at the cost of his freedom, the work he had put in, the missions he accomplished, the families he destroyed, and the lives he had taken meant nothing. All along there were hundreds of others who were putting in the same work and possessed the same status he did.

This enlightenment forces them to realize they have no status. They have been manipulated by the gang which created them. The gang member will realize, once it is too late and their freedom has been taken, that the very walls which have raised them to a level of respect they searched for have now become the walls of solitude.

Standard jail cell

The gang member now understands the people who he set on a pedestal of wisdom and respect have now gone on to recruit yet another "young homie" who can help them continue their reign of terror within the community. Too late to change anything he realizes the "shot callers" of a gang maintain their high status by manipulating another new generation. The gang member worked so hard for the small amount of acceptance, recognition, and status, but ended up in prison. Now that they see how to achieve a higher status and power they will then become the person who manipulates others into worshiping his own status and ideals. The manipulated will become the manipulator, and will find their own generation who will listen to the lies they were once told. The theories and beliefs of what they practiced regarding the gang as a family will no longer exist, at least to them.

The gang member, who wasted much of their life, will use the same powers of manipulation while incarcerated for personal gain. They will claim a life of allegiance and proudly flaunt their tattoos and scars. The gang member will also proudly claim the gang which accepted them using what status they believe they had deserved and earned. They will start yet again, another cycle and generation of human beings looking for the same answers that they had sought many years before.

I once had the opportunity to interview a Mexican Mafia drop out. Ironic that once feared by so many, is an ally in the end. He was an intelligent man with a world of information, strengthening my theories of gang members. He came full circle in his life with what has been described as the inevitable time line of a gang member. He had earned his respect within his gang, raised his level of status as a Mexican Mafia associate, and had given specific instructions on politics and aligning certain areas of the southwest United States. Known throughout the gang community, he was always greeted by fellow gang members as the person who held the keys and would be paid while as long as he was out of prison. However, he was incarcerated and was going to remain so for a good part of his life.

This photograph was discovered during a search warrant and assisted gang detectives in identifying a friendly (clique) gang from a neighboring city. The photograph demonstrated another way of expanding their territory and claiming another gang as their own.

I found our conversation fascinating. I asked, "If you could relive your life would you take the same path knowing what you know now? You were free; why did you continue this lifestyle and not walk away when you had the chance? Why did you choose to continue the lifestyle of a shot caller and work as a liaison to one of the most well-known and feared prison gangs in the United States?" He looked me in the eye and said, "We are not brave enough or smart enough to figure that out. I have never been out long enough to realize how good freedom feels. You listen to what is told to you even though it was never pushed on me. You respect what is ordered and comply with the rules, and when you get to the yard, you always have a choice."

He used my words and ideology regarding choice. What I found odd, was even though the answer appeared as if he would have altered his existence if he could have, the real answer was "This is all I know and what I accept in life, and for me it was the right choice." It edified the reality that such an insignificant level of status within such a small percentage of people can change a person's identity. The answer also strongly indicated that once you have made the "leap of faith" into the gang subculture there is no looking back. You have made a decision for life.

We all have a choice.

Chapter six

Building rapport; the relationship between an officer and gang member

As hypocritical as it may seem, there has to be a common respect between a gang member and a police officer. Respect, not in the sense of understanding the gang members situation and choices, or sympathizing with what excuses the gang members use as a means of manipulation to seek empathy. Let's always remember that we have shown that any gang member, at any time, can stop their pattern of criminal activity and change the lifestyle he or she has chosen. The respect we must acknowledge is an understanding of the pattern of criminal activity and rules this subculture has created over decades of evolution. The police officer can then become more aware of the gang lifestyle. This will assist with the officer's survival and continue to raise their level of expertise and investigative skills within their chosen profession.

As a police officer, you will often hear on countless occasions comments such as, "How can you do this job," or "I could never do what you do." Police officers must develop skills to imprison those who have fraught a reign terror for decades; if they do not take it upon themselves to be society's protector, the senseless acts will continue. Without an understanding of the criminal who commits these crimes and a willingness to put aside their bias and feelings, these crimes go unsolved and the predator continues to prey.

This mentality must be developed to deal with the gang member who for decades have methodically broken down entire cities. Respect for the gang member has to be addressed by the officer or investigator just as one would investigate criminals responsible for the most reprehensible acts that can be imagined. Having an understanding of the subculture, territory, clothing, mentality, dialect, recent crimes committed and self proclaimed monikers, gives the detective a better understanding of who is committing these crimes as well as the most important aspect of law enforcement, officer safety. Having a clear understanding of how the infrastructure of the gang is broken down, the crews involved in committing crimes as well as the mentality and beliefs of a gang member, regardless of the content, excuse, validity or merit, shows the respect level a police officer holds for this subculture. Continued training on a daily basis catapult the knowledge of the every day crimes committed within the area they work. This knowledge can only be gained in one way. **Getting the gang member to talk to you.**

Criminals generally start their lives as everyone else does; attending school, developing a moral foundation within the family structure. Criminals also face social problems like peer pressure and finding an identity. Their attempts to discover their own identity can lead to experimental drug use which can lead to addiction. Other times, the thrill of certain crimes such as theft, robbery, just for monetary gain, can fuel the curiosity of criminal behavior.

There are no rules or training for the common criminal and more often than not, the criminal comes from a family of high moral values, ignorant to crime, drug sales and abuse as well as the rules of criminal sub-cultures. The common criminal is ignorant to the repercussion of criminal behavior. They do not foresee the disasters which will inevitably come and introduce them to the criminal justice system. When they are caught, their true ignorance to the rules of criminal behavior are displayed. The fear of incarceration, the belief they can and will change and deep down inside, the knowledge that what they did was wrong, become self-evident when sitting in front of the detective, admitting to their actions.

The gang subculture is significantly different from the common criminal. Once the gang member makes the decision to subject themselves to this world, the classes start and the training begins. Meetings, personal training, and advice is offered to the gang member as they are propelled into a world of not only criminal behavior, but a world in which the manipulation utilized by the older gang member and their beliefs of community, family, the government, and law enforcement, become the focal point of the training and the gang member is conditioned to lie. The brain washing has begun, and the gang member who accepts this as gospel and believes in its content, changes their views on right and wrong.

The beliefs they are shown by who they perceive as family become their views of what is socially right. Gang member codes and rules become the norm, which are different from the general public. The gang member adopts the deviant theories and abides by them, just as common citizens abide by the rules of society. The language in which the gang member speaks, the rules of respect and pride, become a way of life to the gang member. What one person would think as normal social behavior is looked upon as betrayal to the gang member. This, of course, is in direct opposition to law enforcement who enforce society's rules.

Law enforcement was developed to keep order and protect those who can't protect themselves. Law enforcement officers wear so many hats: they serve as parent, psychiatrist, mentor, and family counselor, perceived as the answer person to all problems within our society. The gang member, due to years of training by the very manipulator they will become, does not view this as socially acceptable, rather the contrary. The gang members have already proven they will not conform to the rules, creating the necessity of law enforcement to fully understand why. Symptoms can only be completely dealt with if the root cause is understood.

Acknowledgment by a gang member and/or accepting law enforcement as an ally in any single incident is a sign of weakness and is not tolerated. Even asking for medical help by a gang member who has been injured due to a violent crime is looked upon with scorn and considered snitching. The incident itself could have been an action of a rival gang or committed by a member of the victims own gang and any cooperation could lead to corroboration on a case. It is not uncommon for a police officer to respond to a violent act and be accosted by members of the gang and its affiliates. Comments to law enforcement such as "We didn't call you we called an ambulance" are not uncommon. This belief of the gang member transforms them into a person of distrust, anger and above all, hatred towards the very people who would help them or their families without judgment.

Law enforcement must understand a gang member's negativity and respect its value. Developing a relationship of common ground is the essential aspect to obtaining the information needed to maintain a level of expertise and knowledge of recent criminal activity. Communication increases the likelihood of awareness of newer members recently accepted by the gang. The law enforcement officer must utilize the same manipulation used by the gang member every day, and channel it as knowledge to be used for the benefit of society. Prejudice, animosity, or anger towards this subculture who commit daily acts of violence and domestic terrorism, can and will cloud the officers ability to obtain the information that is needed to be successful. A police officer creating a gap because of a moralistic hatred towards an ideology and culture, will weaken the boundaries and ultimately benefit the gang.

Failure to obtain knowledge of a gang subculture, dialect, monikers and street terms, can limit your effectiveness on a case if it is determine you are not an expert in a court of law buy a magistrate or judge. Ignorance on the police officers end, or simply refusing to accept the fact this subculture exists, can be the difference between a violent contact with a gang member or a low-key consensual contact in which information is obtained that corroborates and leads to the conclusion of a case.

Law enforcement has learned the community often perceives "kindness as weakness." When it comes to officer safety and going home every night, this saying is valid and justified. There is a fine line within the perception of kindness and respect though. Opposing values in social, parental or religious beliefs, does not give any officer the right to treat anyone disrespectfully. As a human being, regardless of my views of a particular person, I will still shake their hand and acknowledge their existence by saying, "hello." Success for law enforcement, particularly gang detectives is directly linked to the relationships established with gang members; officers must channel their personal emotions into manipulation.

A gang member's life is violent. Reasonable force is a way of life in law enforcement and is essential for survival. We must understand the violent nature in which the gang member has subjected themselves to since their first day of training. A police officer can go their entire career and not shoot one round. A gang member, because of the violence they create every day, can be subjected to a series of incidents and be directly involved on numerous occasions of firing a weapon in a violent incident, both provoked and unprovoked. Violence is what the gang member is accustomed to and is the basis and foundation of their ideology. Intelligence may be considered cowardice in some situations and becomes very uncomfortable for the suspected gang member. The gang member, who has utilized violence due to lack of intelligence, is accustomed to a world of force. Kindness is looked upon as weakness. Respect, is looked upon as a foundation for closing the gap and establishing boundaries between law enforcement and the gang culture. Remember what the ultimate goal is, solving the crime, finding out current trends and getting the gang member to talk to you. This can only be accomplished with communication. Communication leads to intelligence, which leads to convictions and the ultimate goal of placing a predator in prison. Having a clear understanding of who we contact every day will be the difference between failure and success.

Do not allow your personal beliefs, prejudices or egos cloud your judgment of what is best for your investigation. Having a clear understanding of the gang subculture is no different than having knowledge of any culture you come in contact in an area you may be policing. However not essential to be successful as a gang detective, it never hurts when the officer is of the same ethnicity as the gang they investigate and has an understanding due to cultural similarities. Obviously, the officer and gang member do not share the same social ideology; however, they do share common ground regarding culture, language, parental ideology from upbringing. They may also share the family structure of the particular ethnicity. As an example; Asian and Samoan cultures are extremely family orientated in the upbringing of their children. Families being raised with two parents may have decision making conducted by an elder person of the house. By not understanding this culture an officer can unknowingly disrespect the entire family, widening the gap of communication and their ultimate goal, getting the gang member to talk to you.

There are too many stories to count about police officers who grew up in the worst gang infested areas with siblings and parents who were validated gang members and affiliates. These officers were subjected to a life and subculture which, due to their choices, did not become a factor in where they would end up in life. They made the choice because they could see the inevitable and because they decided not to subject themselves to this subculture, became successful in life. Taking the desensitization of a life style and using it as knowledge instead of a life of crime can assist in creating the safest possible community.

Regardless of the officers cultural upbringing playing ignorant to a group of social deviants can break down all lines of communication between the suspected gang member and the interviewer and actually widen the communication gap. As an officer, looking past your comfort level or expertise, even possibly your emotional virtue toward a deviant subculture and analyzing the contents of the subcultures behavior, will create a better understanding of the personality within the gang member you are contacting.

Search and arrest warrants were executed for two gang members during a homicide investigation. Both suspects were transported to jail for interrogation. My partners interviewed the two suspects and the gang members were not cooperating with authorities. I reviewed the property that was confiscated by police during the arrest. The younger suspect had a backpack which contained a notebook with photographs of a female and the suspect in a romantic pose. I also found items related to baseball. I was able to relate to the suspect since I played baseball. I approached the two interrogators and asked if I could speak with the suspect. It is professional etiquette to ask and receive permission from the interrogators to interview their suspect.

My partners had no problem allowing me to speak with the suspect. Murder suspects are complex and traditionally, emotionless and without remorse. They psychologically disassociate themselves from the crime and at times convince themselves they had nothing to do with the death of another human being. In this particular murder the actual target was the victim's father. The victim involved in the confrontation with the suspect had no involvement in their business, but due to a verbal exchange with his father, led to a physical altercation, and then to gun shots. The suspects fled the scene as the victim bled to death in his front yard. Murder crimes are sometimes so heinous they can stir emotions of hatred and animosity toward the killer even from veteran police officers. A police officer must maintain professionalism and control when dealing with deviant individuals. Utilizing the facts of the case to get the suspect to confess and incarcerate a murderer for the safety of all.

The suspect and I made eye contact. He looked at me as if he had a question and he gestured with his head that he wanted to talk to me. His question was inconsequential and I answered him in a friendly, non-threatening manner. I then inquired about the picture I had seen in his notebook. I asked him if the female in the picture was his girlfriend and if so, how long they had been dating? The suspect answered "Yes", and had a somber look as if he missed her already. I mentioned that she is very attractive and how much of a shame it would be if he did not have the opportunity to hold her again. The suspect looked at me as if he agreed, smirked and responded by admitting he loved her. I asked him if he was still active in baseball and if he was part of a team. The suspect looked at me and stated baseball was his passion in high school. We continued the conversation and it was obvious, I had identified with his life. I did not ask questions regarding the murder. The suspect displayed signs of someone who forgot he was in jail for taking a life. I explained my career in baseball and the position I played. I named players who were active in my limited professional career, players he could identify and remember. We talked for about an hour about his life and his relationship with his girl. I explained to him I understood his life and how much of a shame it would be to ruin it with his participation in the murder.

The suspect agreed that he was too young to be involved in a murder. He wasn't the person who pulled the trigger. It was not his idea, nor his plan, and it was not right that he sat in jail for the actions of another. He was only an accomplice to the crime. The suspect looked down, placed his elbows to his knees, and confessed. He described his role involving the death of another human being, the role of the second suspect, and explained where he hid the gun as they fled the scene. Even though he failed to accept full responsibility, he did admit several key elements. We had the right people in custody.

With appropriate communication and interrogation techniques, the gang member confessed to his involvement in the gang and the crimes he committed. Having the knowledge and history of the gang's cultural background, rules, territory, dialect, and the active members who participate in the gang, allows the gang member to have respect for the police officer.

Not withstanding officer safety ever in law enforcement, you can strip away the very personality a gang member uses as a psychological shield they have built through criminal behavior and training in order to combat the person they have perceived as the enemy. This can only be accomplished through intelligence and rapport. Acknowledging a respect level within the subculture and having an understanding of the rules, ethnicity, area, dialect, cultural background and most importantly, the active members involved in the social deviant world of gangs, gives the officer the tools and respectability of the gang member. This respectability level is achieved when the officer has a clear picture of the subculture they are dealing with and an intelligence level which will become feared by the gang member more than aggression.

Even in Law Enforcement, We all have a choice.

Chapter seven

Women and their roles in gangs

While guest speaking at a college criminal justice class, I was asked a question by one of the more intuitive students. "Is it possible to rid the world of gangs, and if so, how could it be done?" I took no time at all in answering the question because I had often thought of how to cripple a gang to extinction? A traditional answer would be, get rid of guns and drugs and take out the source of financial stability related to drug sales and prostitution. Provide more financial aid both state and federal towards educating parents of the importance of gang awareness and prevention. No, that was not my answer. I told the student it was my opinion that if you take females out of the equation and make it socially unacceptable finding nothing attractive about the gang lifestyle, gangs as we know it would quickly disappear.

This gang utilized the bleachers of a high school during school hours for this photo opportunity.

Today's male gang member thrives off of what he can gain from women, using them for everything they can possibly extort. A woman's role, be it knowingly, subconsciously, against her will, or due to ignorance or drug addiction, is literally the foundation of the survival of male gang members. Gang members are pathological and experts at manipulation. They feed off of society and we as a social group allow this to happen.

Society's viewpoint of what is acceptable to one group and not another is difficult to comprehend. When a man molests a child, he is in turn looked at in horror and rage; he is a societal outcast and seen with the ability to manipulate, but by only the innocent and mentally immature. Society says this person is sick, should be executed, and has no right to live in our community. Society as a whole chastises this person and does not allow them to live in peace, because they cannot identify with or understand an individual who could prey on a child, and do the things that result in a lifetime of mental anguish for the victim.

The gang should also be viewed this way when corrupting young females. However, place a moniker, a status symbol, a criminal record, an addiction and a label of a murderer and many people greet it with praise and admiration. He is the American gang member, who's only intentions is to create havoc within a community, oppress the weak, and manipulate the people they encounter. This includes the woman they continuously infect by selfishness, abuse, intimidation, and greed.

The gang member jumps from woman to woman in an effort to raise their own status. This symbolizes the standard of living gang members are accustomed to, which is to take what they want and when they want it. There are no boundaries: age, physical appearance, education level, financial status, mental stability, or criminal history of the female is compared to the status they will gain. A gang member shows no shame when it comes to the manipulation of women and how they use them; in turn, the females continually allow this and have their own measurement of status.

Female Asian gang members flashing their symbol honoring their membership.

I have spoken with hundreds of women during interviews and ask why they would subject themselves to this constant life of abuse, law enforcement contact, and their houses being raided by the police while their children are present. Why, when the gang member has nothing to offer, nor do they contribute anything to society, do they continue to subject them selves to this lifestyle?

Most women do not come to the realization that they are seeking a criminal when developing a relationship, falling in love, and getting married. This mentality is absurd and would be viewed as deviant. However, since the birth of the gang member, those women who live in the social climate that renders gang affiliation acceptable deem a gang member a suitable choice. Women are welcomed into a lifestyle they have a difficult time leaving; It starts innocently enough at the age of curiosity and need for social acceptance, and ends in criminal involvement and conspiracy. These women choose this lifestyle for all the wrong reasons just as women in non-gang related abusive relationships do.

Each female I have spoken to had a different reason for dating a gang member. Here are a few examples: "I love him. I have known him my whole life." "My family was part of a gang." "I thought I could help him. He never acted like that when he was around me."

These reasons or excuses are usually at the tail end of the relationship where children have been conceived. They are manipulated into a thought process which can only be explained by their actions. Depending on the level of involvement and loyalty to the life style they may have an extremely difficult time leaving.

The well known and publicized prison gang **Mexican Mafia** also known as "La Eme" is run by a hierarchy of what is referred to as "Carnales" (Spanish for brothers). They are in charge of the southern portion of Hispanic prison and street gangs. From single man cells, where they are locked down 23 hours a day with no contact with anyone from the outside or other members of the gang. How is it possible a gang can become so powerful and influential with such minimal access or outside contact? Members of the Mexican Mafia have personified the term "manipulation" and survived solely from the loyalty, support, and foundation of women who have demonstrated their undying devotion to the members of this criminal enterprise.

The females are the eyes and ears for these social deviants, literally perpetuating the entire criminal enterprise network from the collection of street level drug taxes, which equates to millions of dollars being passed along to the mafia members and their families. They control all communication between these members throughout the state's prison system. Women will drive hundreds of miles to visit these incarcerated manipulators, all for the sole purpose of providing a gateway and communication network for the members of the gang.

The street level gang and the relationship with females are of the same premise. Gang members who are locked up are constantly looking for a lifeline to the outside, and will use any means possible to communicate. This is easily accomplished through continued criminal enterprise, financial gains, or companionship. The companionship is normally of the sexual nature and used for the gang member's satisfaction and personal selfishness.

The women they involve will spend hours at a prison or county jail, waiting for the fifteen minute visit they get with the gang member they are there to see. They will subject their children to this lifestyle, creating again, a world of generational influence and gang involvement. It is normal for the women who are involved with the gang members to become accustomed to this lifestyle and view it as normal.

Gang members will call upon these women to impeach themselves when it comes to testifying in court, subjecting themselves to criminal prosecution. The well-being of the female does not matter to them. Due to social factors, family abuse, divorce and domestic violence, these women are led to a world of acceptance. Regardless of their beauty, intelligence or education level, financial status or past, these women are manipulated into a world of lies and often, however good their intentions, are subjected to a world of criminal activity at the support of the gang member they love.

As a newly hired officer in 1991, my first unit of assignment was working in a custody facility. The sheriff's department's first priority is staffing the jails and keeping them above minimum state requirements. I was assigned to the men's central jail facility located in downtown Los Angeles. Most of my day was spent dealing directly with gang members.

I developed a questionnaire for gang members who would talk to me. It was centered around the gang member's social life, where they came from, their parents, past convictions, gang territory, descriptions and meaning of their tattoos and why they chose them, financial status, and the obvious, "why did you become a gang member."

Hundreds of gang members spoke to me candidly about their life. Near the end of my tenure I noted an interesting answer from a majority of the gang members, "Why did you become a gang member?" More than 80 percent of them had stated they enjoyed the party aspect and the accessibility to all kinds of women. I did not give it much thought until years later as a gang detective. After thousands of investigations directly related to gangs and violent crime, I found myself not only writing search and arrest warrants for the gang member who committed the crime, but also for the females they were manipulating and living with. In most cases, I was arresting the female for being directly involved with the incident, again subjecting themselves to a life of incarceration and imprisonment. Even though their freedom was taken from them, their children removed by the state and their future in peril, these women stayed loyal.

Women have been tasked with what is referred to as **missions** within the gang structure, as if they were a validated gang member. They are used for stockpiling weapons for the gang and holding drugs for the dealer. The residence they have worked to afford is taken over by the gang and fugitives within the neighborhood are hidden at these locations. These living quarters are an exceptional place to hide from law enforcement because it is not frequented by gang members. The female is used for financial support as well, and usually has a well-paying job or works on a regular basis. Many of these women possess an advanced degree and show their true allegiance to the gang by helping in any way they can.

Females are frequently used as actual crime partners as opposed to years past when they were solely accessories after the fact. The increase in females being named as a suspect is at an all time high, and this is not due to intimidation by the gangster. The females have chosen this life and truly believe it benefits their relationship. The driving of a stolen vehicle to commit acts of violence amongst rival gang members or to conspire to help in commercial robberies is all too common with today's female gang member or associate.

Communication

While gang members are incarcerated, one of the most important aspects they need for their criminal enterprise to thrive is communication with the outside world. Keeping in touch with members of the gang and getting updates on the neighborhood and its politics. Maintaining a line of communication with the female whom they have manipulated into the criminal lifestyle is priority one. Women who have fallen victim to this lifestyle are asked to be the communication conduit for all of the criminal activity which the gang member continues even while they are incarcerated. These women are often referred to by Hispanic gang members as **secretaries.**

One method of assured communication is the use of what is called a **burn out line**. The burn out line is a cell phone fraudulently purchased via the internet utilizing someone's stolen personal information. Gang members know it is extremely easy to purchase this phone line having only the bare minimum of information. Traditionally, the phone is ordered via the internet and delivered in one day to an address near the person who orders the phone. In many cases, the phone line is purchased with a stolen credit card account number in which the purchaser is unidentifiable. The person who orders the phone usually has access to an empty apartment or a triplex housing development which is not being rented. They are aware the phone is going to be delivered to a specific address in one day, so the female who orders the phone, will hang around the empty apartment for the package. Once the delivery is made, the phone is put into use immediately. The phone number is given to the gang member in custody, and the line which has been set up is ordered with many features, such as three way calling, call forwarding, caller ID, and also the capability to accept call waiting.

Now the line of communication has been established. These phone lines are essential for communication within the gang structure--disseminating information throughout the gang as efficiently as an executive secretary. The term "burn out line" means the phone line is used until the phone company has not received a payment and is ultimately burned out when the phone company shuts the line down. These lines of communication are used for all missions within the structure of the gang from family business to witness intimidation, but mostly for the daily criminal activity which occurs within the gang.

In early 2006, I investigated a crime in which three suspects robbed a victim at knife point. I had identified my suspects and authored search warrants for their capture. Once I had arrested everyone involved, my partner Brandt House and I monitored all phone calls from one of the suspect's jail phones. For over a year we noticed that the number the person was calling traced back to a female whose voice was never heard on the phone. It was obvious the phone line had been fraudulently obtained and the people involved had defrauded the victim of over $7,000.00 before the phone company turned it off. The victim, completely unaware her personal information had been used to obtain this phone line, now had an unpaid debt of $7,000.00 on her credit report. This line was used by a gang member to speak with other gang members, attempting to find the victim of the robbery to intimidate him into not testifying. The female who obtained the phone was asked to locate the girlfriend of the victim, so she could be approached by members of the gang in an attempt at intimidation.

The female who obtained the burn out line was the gang member's sister and was arrested for conspiracy to dissuade a witness and identity theft; because of penalties for gang involvement she received 8 years in prison.

Witness Intimidation

Another form of communication utilized by gang members through the use of females is witness intimidation. Witness intimidation does not necessarily come in the stereotypical form that is portrayed in movies. Hollywood's portrayals of organized crime is customarily men of muscle who are sent to locate witnesses and victims and slated to testify against a mob member; they explain through force or intimidation not to testify or cooperate with police during an investigation.

Women are used for intelligence and develop clandestine operations; for example, during a preliminary hearing in a very violent gang case, women from the neighborhood that had no relationship with the suspect were sent to the court room. Again, through a new age of technology they used their cell phones to take pictures and record their testimony of the witnesses as they testified on the stand. Using women for this form of intimidation is done for several reasons. Male gang members know when they walk into a court room they are opening themselves up for contact with police. More times than not, the gang members are on parole or probation, making themselves subject to search and seizure at any time. Also, many of them have strict gang conditions regarding their parole and probation and can not be seen with other gang members in any forum.

The idea is to send an unassuming person who has no personal or family ties to the charged individual. What better way to infiltrate this process than the seemingly non-threatening female. She walks in without flare or suspicion, abides by all rules of the court room and does not bring any attention to herself. She becomes the actress she always wanted to be as being excused from the court room would result in not being able to finish the mission. She wears conservative clothes and goes unnoticed as she prepares to execute her assignment. She is alone, but mixed with the audience who are awaiting unrelated cases to be called by the judge. She is given specific orders to record, write down or memorize the day's events. Then, she is to relay these events during the course of the day to gang members from the neighborhood. Decisions of consequences are made when someone has testified against the gang and betrayed their views.

These women are usually unattractive compared to the standards society has deemed attractive. They are chosen for a reason. They are messengers, using the latest technology to show their allegiance to their neighborhood.

Selected profession as a Resource

These women have not only been used for the purposes of revenge and intimidation, but also for their professions. They are often placed strategically in areas for the sole purpose of furthering the enterprise of the gang. Throughout my tenure in gang investigations, I have investigated numerous females who were directly affiliated, if not a jumped in member, of the gang. During these investigations, I have discovered many of these women play the role of the mole, working in an area with access to personal files of both the unaware citizen and law enforcement. For decades, the Mexican Mafia has had access to personal files through the DMV, loan offices, medical offices, and hospitals. These women are used for their access to information as well as their paycheck. It initially appears to these women that only a few people will be victimized by stolen information, until the residence of an unsuspecting witness in a pending court case is given to the gang. It occasionally ends in murder.

A strategically placed woman in a position to access confidential information can assist in dismissals of court cases by retrieving information for the gang. There have been many missing cases and false dispositions at both police departments and the district attorney's office.

I was involved in a case regarding a Mexican Mafia affiliate. His job, once he was released from prison, was to collect taxes from drug dealers who sold drugs in the neighborhood that was governed by the Mexican Mafia. He was to help align the gang in a more profitable enterprise and show he was the person making every decision within the gang, **holding the keys**. While this subject was re-aligning the gang, he was arrested for being a convicted felon in possession of a gun. We knew where he was living and the female he was living with and executed a search warrant at the residence.

During our search I found hundreds of personal profiles of unsuspecting victims which the female had obtained through her job; an online, paperless medical insurance company. This female obtained employment at this company for the sole purpose of stealing the personal profiles of people who had signed up for medical insurance. She then used the profiles as financial means to obtain internet-purchased items.

I contacted the female's employer and was not surprised to hear how they described the female's personality and work ethic. The management was shocked to hear about the arrest because they thought she was so nice and personable towards the customers. She never showed any delinquency or negative issues at work and was liked by everyone in the office. They stated they would have never believed she was someone linked to a gang, let alone someone directly linked to the **Mexican Mafia**. Her paycheck from the company, which was turned over to the gang, was not nearly as important to the gang as the access to personal information used by this medical insurance company. A simple click of the computer opened a wealth of personal information and allowed the suspect full access to any medical record on file. In this case, the computer system had been accessed on numerous occasions.

Women are not only used for their finances, they are also used in the form of law enforcement. The background investigation process to get into law enforcement can be grueling. It can take months on end and depending on the amount of people authorized by the police agency to hire and a time frame in which the hiring police departments are given. Due to time pressure background investigators sometimes overlook certain key issues about a person's background and lifestyle. Gang-linked women have infiltrated law enforcement for many years. Sometimes, these women were placed in positions at law enforcement agencies for the sole purpose of access to personal information.

It is difficult for gang members to infiltrate the hiring process to be police officers (although it does happened) due to the numerous safeguards built in. However, civilian and non sworn positions have lesser standards and for the most part do not require psychological and polygraph examinations. The gang also encourages the females to obtain advanced degrees in criminal justice and find employment at any law enforcement agency that will hire them.

In 2006 my partner Brandt House and I were monitoring phone conversations from a visiting area of a jail between a gang member and a female who claimed the same gang as the one responsible for killing my friend and partner Jerry Ortiz. It was during this session that I heard one of the most horrendous comments we had ever heard during a conversation between a female and a gang member.

The conversation started off innocently enough. The gang member attempted to coax the female into a sexual phone conversation; general conversation with nothing of evidentiary value toward our case. Then the conversation changed and the gang member verbalized his disgust at the deputies who worked at the jail. As he said this, the female answered, "That's why we kill them out here." I knew she was referring to the death of my friend and hero of the community, Deputy Jerry Ortiz.

It was shocking that a woman who had never had a run-in with law enforcement or had even been detained could proudly spew out those evil words. That someone could take such pleasure in mocking the very person that at some point helped her or her family members stay safe. I was overcome with emotion. I continued to listen to the conversation, and heard the female gloat of the college she was attending; she explained to the gang member how she was going to obtain a position in law enforcement, possibly as an officer or for the probation department. This seemingly innocent female had been completely brainwashed by this gang member who had spread his hatred for law enforcement to her. She blindly mocked the murder of a hero she had never met and took pride in the gang who had widowed a new bride and left children fatherless. I had to know who this person was and learn why such vitriolic words could come from her.

Legally, she did nothing wrong, but I could not listen to these hateful words without becoming curious to the true cause of her hatred. I checked the gang member's jail visiting records and attempted to verify the female's identity through a system's check. I used every aspect of investigative knowledge I had and came up with nothing. She had no criminal history and had never been identified as a gang member or even an affiliate. I finally found her in the local high school records and discovered she had recently graduated. She lived in a city plagued and infested by gangs. I knew her name, I knew where she lived, and I knew what college she went to, but I also knew she had not committed any crimes other than the crime of ignorance, selfishness and disgracing human ethics. I held onto the information, which, exactly one year later would pay off and change the female's life forever.

Chapter eight

There is always someone listening!

In November of 2007, I was a part of one of the largest gang injunctions in Los Angeles County, which was aimed at a local gang. The gang injunction was pursued by a tenacious and hard working district attorney named Deanne Castorina. She was a beautiful woman who was professional and extremely knowledgeable about her work. Deanne was ruthless in her pursuit of civil action and submitted the affidavit; she presented to the court an 800 page declaration and legal argument revealing the seriousness of the criminal behavior of this gang.

The concept was simple; conditions of the injunction were not to be violated by members or affiliates of the gang who had been served with the injunction. The injunction included any and all members of the gang who were observed by law enforcement violating specific safety zones. The injunction met legal challenges and each of the gang members were served with specific conditions and subject to immediate arrest.

On one occasion, Los Angeles County Deputies were dispatched to a party in the same gang-infested area that was subject to the civil injunction. The party was like any other gangster party: Gang members puffing their chests in the street, high from the methamphetamine which fueled their egos. Women, drunk and obnoxious were yelling at the deputies as they continued to make some sort of order out of the chaotic event. Several people were detained for curfew, drinking in public, and gang injunction violations. One female was served with the gang injunction condition form due to her obvious affiliation.

The party was dispersed and several people were arrested. Several weeks after the party, I was contacted by Deputy District Attorney Deanne Castorina by telephone. She told me she had been contacted by a professor from a local college that specialized in criminal justice. The professor had inquired about the gang injunction because one of her high achieving criminal justice students had been served and she was worried the service would hurt her chances of obtaining a position in law enforcement. Deanne said the professor wanted to know who she could speak to about this problem, because she had hopes of somehow redeeming the girl's reputation and future. It was fairly common for people who had been served, or their parents, to call and inquire; I am always willing to listen to someone who wants to speak with me about their gang affiliation. When Deanne told me the name, I realized that it was the same girl who a year prior, laughed, joked and disgraced the very meaning of the word "officer", as she spewed the words, "That's why we kill them out here."

I decided to meet with this professor and the female so we could shed some light on her true intentions of entering law enforcement. We set up a meeting with the professor who was grateful, unknowingly setting herself up for a conference that would change her views of gangs. She would soon be a first-hand witness to gang infiltration and the true role of females in the gangs.

My partner Brandt House, Deanne, and I drove to the college. I remember students watching me with curiosity as we approached the office. You see my look is not one of a traditional police officer. I resemble, at times, the very people I investigate. I wear jeans to work, a black t-shirt with a funny or politically incorrect anecdote printed on the front. I stand five foot eleven inches tall and weigh 210 pounds. My head is shaved, but my face is not. My addiction to tattoos is evident with ink protruding from underneath my short sleeve T-shirts. I understood their curiosity. As we walked in, I shook the hand of the professor who I knew would attempt to exonerate her star student.

Setting the stage for what was to come, I introduced myself to the female student calling her by her gang nickname. Her expression made it clear that she was scared and wondering how this stranger knew her nickname.

The professor sensed her discomfort and excused herself to speak with a colleague. She re-entered the room with her colleague, who introduced himself as the director of administration for the criminal justice program, and asked to sit in on the meeting. I gladly told the head of administration, "What the hell, the more the merrier."

Always being the interrogator, I strategically placed the female's chair in front of me taking away her comfort zone. I made sure the professor and head of administration were in back of us so the female was not able to make eye contact with them. I wanted her full attention without distractions. Knowing I was dealing with a professor of law who had worked as a public defender prior to becoming an instructor, I explained to the girl that she was not involved in a criminal investigation, therefore, her Miranda Rights were not an issue regarding self incrimination. I explained that I was attending this meeting because her professor had asked me to explain the reason she had been served with the gang injunction.

I asked the girl if she knew a certain gang member (the same one she spoke to while he was in custody) and what their relationship was. The female said that she knew him, but they were just friends, all the while refusing to look me directly in the eyes. I asked her if she had ever written to the male gang member while he was incarcerated, and she admitted that she had written to him, but only a couple of times.

I then retrieved more than 20 letters and showed them to the female. I had confiscated these letters from the gang members cell (state law allows law enforcement personnel to confiscate, read, or use as evidence without warrant any letter or written paraphernalia by a person in custody). I told the female, "A little bit more than just a couple, don't you think." As she solemnly nodded her head the professor was in disbelief and obvious embarrassment. The professor then voiced her disgust for the female, explaining to her that she had placed her professional name at risk by agreeing to meet with law enforcement.

I then told everyone in the room that I had recorded a phone conversation between the girl and a gang member and wanted to play the recording. Before I did this, I moved closer to the female and placed a photograph in front of her. The photograph depicted Jerry Ortiz and another Deputy Sheriff Tim Brennan. Tim and Jerry were partners who worked the gang enforcement team together. On one occasion Jerry and Tim helped catch three suspects who had just car-jacked a female. Because of circumstances and bravery surrounding the event and arrest, they were awarded with the Medal of Valor. This picture showed Jerry and Tim smiling as they held their awards; the student showed no emotion as she looked at it. I played the tape recording and as I did this, it became evident to the professor exactly what type of person they had attending their college. Even the administrator understood what she intended to cultivate with the education they were providing her and what her role is as a female within a gang.

The professor was outraged when the infamous statement played on the tape, "That's why we kill them out here." I then explained to both the administrator and the professor that they had been fooled by a **mole.** A person who was going to use any means available to benefit the gang through intelligence, financial or sexual means.

I told everyone in the room to look at the female's "death stare". This is the common facial response of a gang associate when questioned. There was no emotion, no tears, no fear, no sorrow, no disgrace nor an apology. I told the girl all I wanted was an apology to the family, to law enforcement, and maybe to me, but she continued her death stare. In retrospect, I did not know what I wanted from this meeting other than to expose the very evil which resides in our lives every day and continues to infiltrate our community.

The administrator shook my hand with sorrow, gratitude, and an apology, almost as if the school was to blame. The female sat in her chair, shoulders slumped, but still nothing in her eyes and a vacant soul. I looked down at her and said, "Good luck in life," and we left.

Later that night after everyone else had gone home, I sat in my office working; my phone rang, it was the professor from earlier in the day. In an emotional tone she told me how thankful she was for bringing this to her attention and apologized for the event. I told her it was not her fault and she ended the conversation by saying, "we felt it was in the best interest of the college that she not attend our institution any longer." To this day I keep in contact with the professor and will always consider her a dear friend.

Criteria and General Characteristics

Not all women who become involved with gang members and gang enterprises were brought up in the lifestyle or even raised in areas where they would be exposed to gangs. I have noticed a very close correlation to the women who are involved with gangs, and the mental, physical and social aspects in which the female was raised. Low levels of self-confidence and self worth, certain physical appearance, lack of a father figure, generational gang family members, and abuse have played a significant role in a gang member's choice of the female. The decisions females have made when it comes to involvement with gang members, often begins as it does with any teenager looking for acceptance within her age group. Photographs of female gang members at a young age show the same characteristics as those of a normal generation. Parties, drinking, mild drug use, camaraderie, prom pictures, and whatever else is popular to gain acceptance with peers. The people depicted in these photographs show the same social characteristics one would classify as normal social behavior. But what about the female who has not been raised in a so-called generational family climate of gangs? There are literally millions of women who fall into this manipulative trap that takes over their lives and they are mentally too weak to make the decision of walking away. It is not uncommon for these women to have been raised with a fundamentally strong foundation.

How are these women found? In many cases, these women are educated and raised with good values. They keep normal jobs and continue to feed the ego of the gang member by enabling them to continue their criminal behavior. Male gang members possess the ability of manipulation to the highest degree. What one has to remember is the psychological make up of a gang member is that of a sociopath. They lie, cheat and steal without remorse. The extreme need for acceptance and status is so overwhelming the gang member will say and do whatever is necessary to achieve his goal.

The gang member is searching for status by any means and selfishness takes precedent over the feelings of anyone or anything. The gang member seeks out a female of low self esteem, physically inferior in comparison to society's standards, and who can not seem to find an identity. This is referred to as social engineering and utilized by the more sophisticated gang member. Social engineering within the gang is when the gang member identifies potential flaws and assets in a female's personality who has been targeted and is susceptible to manipulation. They tell the female what she wants to hear, in hopes they will get what they are looking for. This occurs frequently with gang members who are incarcerated. They are constantly looking for the **hook up** as it is referred to. Women will feed the very same ego that will take over her life and slowly dismantle it. It is almost automatic for male incarcerated gang members to claim to have found God and claim to have changed. They have 24 hours a day to think of ways of manipulating others into ultimately getting their way. They do not care about a woman's physical appearance, and they will seek the female who feels as if they are physically unattractive. The gang member will lure a female who naturally believes people can change, and whose motherly instincts will make them vulnerable. The female they choose is prey to the gang member and used in the most inhumane and manipulative ways.

My partner and I traced a member of the Mexican Mafia who had been tasked with the position of tax collector made from proceeds of drug distribution from the neighborhood. His job was to collect money from all parties that were selling drugs in a specific area and send the proceeds to the **Carnal**. The carnal who hired him vouched for the tax collector's character which established credibility and the ability to collect, temporarily "holding the keys."

We conducted a surveillance of several residences the soldier was related to and noted one in particular. The residence was approximately 60 miles from our location. A city mixed with gang members and Mexican nationals who were hard working people looking for a better life. Every law enforcement systems check showed the residence was clean. In fact, after speaking with law enforcement officials from the area, we found out the residence was linked to a generational family regarding retail ownership in the city dating back to the 50's. The family was known in the community as giving and sympathetic to those who were not so financially fortunate. Interestingly enough, it was not the first time we had seen financial fronts for the Mexican Mafia, businesses set up for the laundering of money for the benefit of financial gain.

We were able to ascertain that one of the people who lived at the location was in fact the current wife of the suspect we were looking for. Oddly enough, there was no criminal history at all when I researched the wife, not even a ticket. The wife was clean and members of her family showed no criminal history at all. I spoke with local law enforcement officers in charge of their gang unit. They were not surprised about the investigation; after years of seeing the worst in our line of work, there really is not too much that surprises us. But in this case, there were a lot of questions--questions I was willing to answer.

A multiple location search warrant was authored and this residence was added to the list. I was in charge of meeting with members of the local police department, who were grateful enough to provide an entry team and help search the residence.

Departments often share resources, such as entry teams.

An **early morning wake up call** was about to be made on the occupants of yet another unsuspecting residence. As I watched the team suit up in their entry gear, I was contacted by one of the team members. He explained to me his knowledge of the people who lived at the residence and wanted to know how, in fact, a direct associate of the Mexican Mafia has any relationship to the people of this residence. He said he has worked the area for years and knows the people who live at the house intimately. He said the people who lived at the house, including the target female and wife to our suspect have all worked for the family business and have been active in the community. I told him that I knew nothing of the family other than a confirmation of one of the occupants of the house, which was in fact, the wife of a Mexican Mafia associate.

I commiserated with the officer's attempt to protect the woman's reputation as I understood how he felt. I explained a theory which had been corroborated too many times to count in my years as a gang investigator. We looked at a photograph of the wife, who was heavy set, not attractive to the rules of what society has instilled for decades, had no criminal record, and was a home grown girl which only added to the profile of a female gang associate. I guessed that her upbringing had been strict, conservative, and structured. I told the officer I theorized she met our suspect while he was in custody, constituting a standard **hook up**. Traditionally these types of people are called pen pals, but let us call them what they are, **facilitators**; women who are manipulated into financially supporting those who are incarcerated.

When you author and serve a search warrant, there is always the uneasy feeling just before the first knock on the front door. Second guessing yourself with questions like, are we hitting the right house? Will my suspect be at the location? Will there be a shooting? Fortunately on this day our hard work, tenacity, and investigation skills paid off; our female was home, and it was the right female. All the occupants of the residence were detained without any problems. Once the entry team began their search, I introduced myself to the female I was there to see. She displayed the personality traits I had seen a hundred times before from a hook up, a meek personality and devotion to her son she cradled in her arms. As in all my cases, my job as the investigating officer is to contact all parties who have been detained and explain without compromising the investigation, the reason for our visit.

I placed my hand on her shoulder and with a solemn, but convincing voice I told her she was not under arrest, but I needed to speak to her. I had a family member take her son and escorted her to another room. I spoke with her in general terms, explaining I could not tell her the essence of our investigation, but would answer her questions when the time came. I showed her a photograph of the man we were searching for. She acknowledged the photo and stated the man depicted was her husband. She explained to me that she and her husband had separated; more so, he just left, abandoning her and their son.

I asked her how she met the suspect, and she said she met her husband from a female friend of who cut her hair. The hairdresser had a boyfriend who was in state prison and his cell mate, her future husband, was looking for someone to "write to". She said the suspect said all the right things to her and made her feel special, like no one else ever had. She believed he had changed while in custody and was looking for a way out. I asked her if she was aware of his past and the reason he was incarcerated. She told me, "He always said it was better that I didn't know." The female acknowledged the fact her husband and the focal point of our investigation was an active gang member and even knew what his moniker was. Yet she still exposed herself to his lifestyle and ultimately gave birth to his child. It is ironic how people can subconsciously become the person they originally despised.

Violent crimes are what fuel the soul of the gang member and blacken the heart of society. Drive-by shootings, armed robbery, drug sales, and even kidnapping are a part of my everyday life of investigations. In the past and traditionally, the standard rule was that females were not allowed on a mission. She was not kept in the loop to criminal actions in the streets between gang members and their prey. It wasn't that the females couldn't be trusted; it was a man's world and an unwritten code. The female was used sparingly, more for sexual gratification and to fuel the ego of the gang member. Criminal behavior and violent acts now includes females.

We as detectives are not only looking for the male shooter in a drive by shooting, but the female driver as well. Drug sales and transportation are not run by the "shot caller" in the neighborhood anymore; in fact, the female role is what we refer to as a **ruse**, a deflection to law enforcement. The theory is why would a cop notice a female driver, or why would the police officer believe this woman who appears to be of no threat be a potential "good stop"? The term "crime partner" has manifested into the female role related to gangs and more times than not, the female is the person we are looking for. The girlfriends, the wife, even the sister. The gang member has become a psychological menace to the world around them by using mind games as a strategy towards manipulation. The gang member uses terms such as "my wife", or they will ask to be referred to as the "king".

They prey on the woman's background and past experiences as a psychological foundation to ultimately strive for their objective. The women serve various purposes, such as placing money on the gang member's personal prison accounts personal books while incarcerated, commonly referred to as placing money **on the books**. Further they are asked to give false testimony in court proceedings to free him. Women also carry out missions for communication with other gang members and family members; stockpiling drugs and weapons, and fulfilling personal hook ups for sexual gratification both while on the streets as well as while the gang member is incarcerated.

Letters

They will tell the female they have found God and use verses from the bible, all the while continuing their game of cat and mouse with law enforcement, which they know is reading correspondence. As part of my investigations I read mail which I have confiscated from gang members and their incarcerated female crime partners.

The female, yearning for a better life, a life without abuse, drug addiction, molestation, or just a male figure which was taken from them by the same lifestyle they have chosen, will listen to the words of her husband and become the very thing she wanted to get away from for so many years. The letters are an easy way to continue the manipulation of the female. The female writes of a desire for a better life, a life with a picket fence and children. I read a letter where the female wrote of her dream of being with this gang member in a "normal world." She authored a very descriptive letter of what she could see as a future life together. Despite this heartfelt desire, the male always wrote with a different agenda. He constantly referred to how much time he had left and his unsatisfied outlook of his future; he would constantly mention how angry he was that she had spoken to the police during an interview and gave incriminating statements.

The game is simple; the female is used for the benefit of the gang and the gang member. During an investigation of a male gang member who I arrested with his girlfriend who was a gang member with the female clique of the gang, I confiscated the letters they had in their cell while both of them were in custody. I was not surprised that what I read gave a clear understanding to the mentality of the female and the manipulation of the male gang member who had, in his words, "found God." The following is an excerpt taken verbatim from these letters showing the manipulation of the gang member and the ignorance of the female:

Letter from the male
"I like the quote from, The Enduring heart that reminds you of me. It is so, and even more so than it's quote. When I think of you I feel it deep in my stomach of my soul. Im sorry for failing us, and not securing our future. Do good my love you are everything my heart desired and more. I don't feel like a hero when you hide things from me. Be good my queen as I am your king, I love you your husband.

At the time I confiscated this letter, I also found two other letters from the same gang member addressed to different woman proclaiming this same allegiance to them. Further, at the end of one of the letters it stated:

"P.S. I need stamps and envelopes, I have no money on my books so if you could ask your uncle to put some money on my books, I wud apreseate it."

The following is a verbatim excerpt from a letter taken from the female who was the so-called "wife" of the male who wrote to her;

She writes: "what do you mean you question my love to you, I am in jail because of the love I have for you, I am willing to go to prison, because of the love I have for you, I am even willing to testify and lie, just because I love you, I understand we have not been together for a while and the bars hold us from each other but you make me sad wen you question me like that. I didn't do anything wrong, yes I talk to homy's from the neighborhood but not like that, let me ask you something, do you talk to any girls besides me."

The manipulation by the gang member affects women of all races and ethnicities and most will end in incarceration, loss of family members and loss of their children to the system and child services. They take the word of the gang member as gospel and continue to subject their own freedom and ownership of their children to the gang member they refuse to let go.

Reality is that there does seem to be a common characteristic and psychological profile of the female who constantly exposes herself to the gang life. The gang member seeks out a female who has been plagued by obesity, as many women who struggle with their weight suffer from low self esteem and fall prey to the manipulator.

In addition these women battle with self-worth and social acknowledgment, many suffered from molestation, abuse both physical and mental, and the all too often broken home. Many are mothers who jump from boyfriend to boyfriend, dealing with their own social and physiological problems, which in turn, create the revolving door affect of generational female gang members or associates. The female feels because of the social surroundings she has been accustomed to she has no where to go and is drawn to those who do not pass judgment on them because of a physical flaw or a limited level of education.

The problem also becomes cultural. Immigrants who come to this country looking for a better way, a better future for their families, almost enable this behavior because of the generation gap and unwillingness to learn from a country that provides so much. The parents do not understand this lifestyle, which economically forces their families into believing they have made the right choice geographically. This ends up being the downfall of their female children who are struggling with acceptance of her peers.

I was once involved with an investigation involving Asian gang members, which leads me to the service of several search warrants. The target involved was the girlfriend of a gang member who had recently been incarcerated for another senseless violent crime. During the service of the warrant, I searched the female's room. I found correspondence and photographs from gang members, male and female, which left no doubt about her affiliation with a gang. I spoke to the mother who told me she thought it was a club. She knew all of her daughter's friends and she had straight A's in high school and had nothing to do with gangs. I explained each photo and what the gang signs and symbols meant, but it fell on deaf ears. The mother refused to believe her daughter would be part of a lifestyle she so despised.

A contemporary breed of female in gangs who knowingly and willingly participate in gang crimes as facilitators has emerged. They view gangs as a status mobility system and hope to achieve the status of secretary. The female places herself in these positions with the hope of developing a relationship with a shot caller. The women who develop relationships with the shot caller are considered royalty in the gang world. A female facilitator for a Mexican Mafia Member holds the same elevated nobility of the position as the carnal himself.

Age as a Factor

Age and maturity level can be a huge factor in the female role and their decision to be part of a lifestyle that ultimately steals their freedom. The male gang member preys on the young. They seek out young females who fall into the anti-social role of acceptance within their peers and their schools. They want what every female teenager wants, to be loved, accepted, found attractive, and most of all, to be given self-worth. The morals and values that the female was raised with determine the female's standards, which in terms of gang member prey are very low. Just the simple acknowledgment they are alive can satisfy what the female is looking for and the male gang member knows it.

The gang member preys on the young female who is either not mature enough to fully understand the situation, or is eager for attention due to abuse of some kind at an early age. It is fairly common for a 24 year old male gang member to be corresponding with a 15 year old female. Again, it starts off as a curiosity, and the female does not understand she has been chosen to be the next victim to fall into the grasp of the neighborhood. They will also be encouraged by other females who have fallen prey to the gang member; this encouragement from other females justifies their existence as an associate to the gang and increases their willingness to do whatever it takes to continue in this life of being needed.

I was assigned a case where deputies had come across a garage full of gangsters. It was a standard mobbing by the neighborhood thugs. As the deputies entered the garage, one male gang member in particular stood out from all the rest. He was a parolee who had been to state prison on more than one occasion. He was known as being sinister in his ways and down for his gang and the furtherance of its promotion. In this garage the deputies saw him lying in a bed with a young female lying across his body, wearing only a shirt. Her naked body was exposed from the waist down and it was obvious to the deputies what was going on. The gang member was 25 years old and respected by fellow members. The girl was 14 years old and had been passed around plenty of times. The gang member was arrested for child molestation and the female was taken into protective custody.

I happened to recognize the girl from an interview from a previous drug possession arrest. We spoke about the circumstances surrounding the arrest of who she referred to as "her boyfriend." She told me he treated her well and would let her come over and shower whenever she wanted and that he would always feed her. She bragged that he had bought her McDonalds that day. It was a small price to pay I guess for the gang member's sexual gratification. The young girl has been conditioned to believe this was the standard based on what she has already been exposed to at an early age. In this particular circumstance, the level and expectation was not high. In fact, only the cost of water for a shower and a hamburger transformed this female into anything the gang member wanted her to be. We all have a choice, and it was her choice to be involved in that lifestyle.

Chapter nine

CHILDREN ARE CONTINUOUSLY EXPOSED TO THE GANG CULTURE

An after funeral party. Notice the child with the same hair style and clothed in the same gang attire.

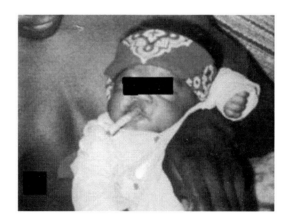

Parental ignorance at its finest.

Young gang member already demonstrating loyalty to the gang.

Twelve year old proudly displaying gang sign with seemingly no disapproval from adult figure

Gang member smoking marijuana while child plays next to him.

Three adults proudly watch the youngster display a gang sign.

Indoctrination

Gang tattoos

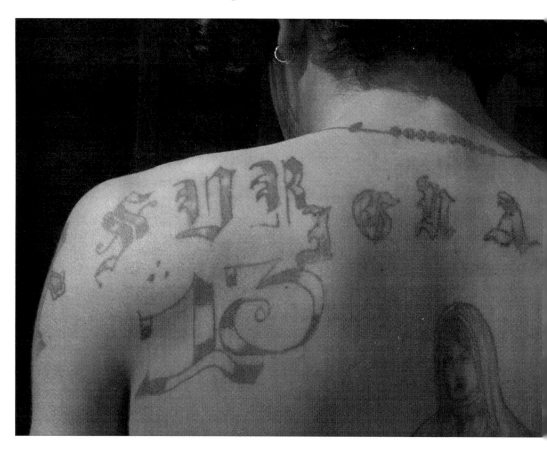

SUR (Sureno- Southsider) a common symbol among Hispanic gang members honoring the Mexican Mafia. The letter 13 denotes the 13th letter of the alphabet, which is "M" also signifying the Mexican Mafia.

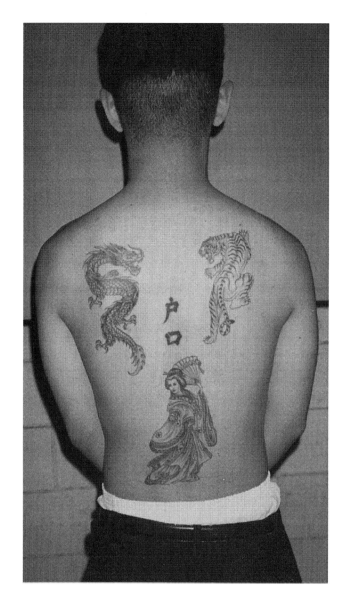

Asian gang tattoos.

Gang graffiti

*Gang members proudly pose for a photograph in a local park. Notice the names on the upper left and bottom right of the wall, known as a **roll call**. Traditionally, names within graffiti represent the gang members responsible and/or present at the time the graffiti was committed. Historically the first name listed, is the person who actually sprayed or marked the graffiti.*

Graffiti on abandoned house is another form of taking over neighborhoods and spreading fear in the community.

A traditional roll call commonly found inside their own residence.

Letters representing a rival gang will be crossed out. For example, if the author is depicting his own name of "GARY" through graffiti and a rival gang begins with the letter "A" Gary will cross out the letter "A" within his own name.

Graffiti utilizing the actual hand sign in an effort to spread continued intimidation in the neighborhood.

A constant reminder to law enforcement.

Graffiti does not always have overt threats. Sometimes it is simply utilized to mark the territory the gang claims within a neighborhood.

Numerous gangs making a statement on whom they are at war with, as well as claiming the area. It may be impossible to determine which gang scribbled graffiti first without corroborating events or intelligence.

More neighborhood intimidation.

Law Enforcement

Early morning wake up call. Briefing for multiple search warrant service.

On occasion we will serve numerous search warrants simultaneously in several counties. Outside agencies assist each other when there is a need. This allows law enforcement to serve the warrants at the same time to minimize the safety risk of prior communication between gang members.

Deputy District Attorney Mike Enomoto

Detective Gary Sloan (center, arms crossed) "With the finest investigative team I have ever worked with."

Ready for Battle

Gang members showing off.

Gang members use the excuse of needing to "protect the neighborhood", but who are they really protecting?

Would you ever think these two females had the capability and means to kill you?

Confiscated weapons during an "early morning wake up call".

Additional weapons found during a multi-location search warrant.

Gang Members being "Jumped in".

Asian gang member being "jumped in".

This photo captured from a videotape of a female gang initiation. Often it appears as if the participants are laughing; this is due to the euphoria of the event and the fact a large percentage of the gang members are under the influence of alcohol and drugs.

Male gang member in the background videotaping the event.

GANG MEMBERS PAYING TRIBUTE TO THEIR NEIGHBORHOOD

Gang members at the neighborhood park with children playing in the background.

Gang members again utilizing local neighborhood park for meetings and photo opportunity

Female Asian gang members proudly displaying their sign. The graffiti in the background may or may not be theirs. Asian gangs are typically not territorial.

As stated before, whoever holds the cash holds the power. However, that power is ALWAYS short-lived.

Male and female gang members interacting and posing for photograph. Note the male and female working together to form a gang sign.

Chapter ten

Divided Lines: The social breakdown of drugs and gangs, and the communities they destroy

I refer to this chapter of the book as "divided lines" because drugs, coinciding with the rise of the criminal street gang have become the forefront of financial gain. What people have not taken into consideration is that the very thing which brings a gang together, is the same force which divides it. This is not specific to gangs and its members; it also tears down the foundation of a community leaving people prisoners in their own homes.

Gangs make millions from drug sales

Crack cocaine hit the streets in the early 1980's, and has not only ruined millions of lives, but has generated financial gains for the benefit of the gang; reaching in the billions. Black, White, Asian and Hispanic gangs all profit from drug sales, although ultimately it was responsible for their individual demise and a source of their imprisonment. President Ronald Reagan passed a tough on drugs doctrine making all laws directly related to crack cocaine a felony with stiff penalties for a conviction.

GANG MEMBERS MAKE MONEY BY UTILIZING THESE TOOLS OF THE TRADE

Confiscated ingredients from a clandestine methamphetamine lab. Entering one of these labs is extremely dangerous due to the volatility of the ingredients.

Finished methamphetamine product

Cocaine in powder form

This is the purest form of cocaine. The impurities (cut) have been cooked away. It has formed what is referred to in the street as "rock" or "crack", but is technically called base cocaine.

The most common weights and terminology are listed below:
Nickel- .05 grams
Dime- .1 grams
Twenty- .2 grams
Sixteenth- 1/16 of an ounce, 1.75 grams
Eight ball- 1/8 of an ounce, 3.5 grams
Ounce- 28.5 grams

Piece of tar heroin. This narcotic has a strong odor of vinegar.

Communities were taken over by the sales of crack cocaine and were held at bay by the gangs who were running the drug enterprise. Families were not allowed to let their children play outside. Sales of home security systems quadrupled due to the huge rise of residential burglaries. Citizens of the community could no longer trust the insufficient law enforcement resources that were dealing with financial struggles of their own. Paranoia, confusion, lack of trust, and fear spread throughout communities paving a way for a completely different force that was about to show itself. This force would be an epidemic consistent with the AIDS virus; not only in terms of destruction, but also that it would be incurable. This force was deemed methamphetamine.

During World War II, a drug was developed by the Japanese that would allow employees to withstand the rigorous hours of factory work and help pilots over come long bouts of sleep deprivation for combat purposes. A so-called *super drug* developed by scientists to aid in an on-going fight against the United States to ensure victory.

Methamphetamine is not a new drug at the street level. Outlaw motorcycle gangs have used it as a source of income since the late 1970's. It is a stimulant drug made from the most common of household and industrial chemicals; it has an affect on people in excess of ten times the potency of crack cocaine. It has the ability to alter the brain's capacity of producing certain chemicals which balances our central nervous system. This super drug that was created has mutated into what is referred to as the **devil,** because it has no cure, no medication, and no hope for some 95 percent of people who use it.

This addiction is like no other and can only be fueled by the drug itself. Continued use of methamphetamine will result in the brain discontinuing its production of chemicals such as dopamine, a chemical released to the body which helps the central nervous system differentiate its emotions. Therefore the only chemical allowing the brain to function normally would now be **methamphetamine**.

Finished product (methamphetamine)

Base (rock, crack) cocaine packaged for quick and easy transactions.

Tar heroin packaged for quick and easy transactions.

Heating a narcotic and loading the syringe.

I have been involved in some of the most horrendous, unthinkable crime investigations, where methamphetamine was the cause of the suspect's actions. However, there have been no studies to my knowledge of crimes committed and the relation of the suspect's methamphetamine abuse at the time of the crime. In fact a study like this would be impossible as every individual arrested would need to submit to a blood test. Through thousands of investigations my conclusion is the link of methamphetamine and part I crimes (part I crimes are defined as crimes against persons ranging from criminal homicide to arson) is around an astounding 70 to 80 percent.

I have been fortunate in my career to have been invited to local colleges as a guest speaker. In one of the class segments I tell the students the same question that I impose upon the reader. If you are a mother, imagine the love for your child; if you are married, imagine the love for your spouse; if these do not apply, then imagine the love for your family. Now I want you to feel the depth of your love for your family. The euphoria you experienced derived from the central nervous system and the release of a chemical produced in the brain (endorphins). Now imagine that you could never voluntarily experience that same feeling again, unless it was chemically manufactured. This is a force which has altered your personality and brain function to the point where only the ingestion of a chemical stimulant will allow the brain to feel the same euphoric effect, which used to be triggered by the people we love and the positive moments that occur in our lives every day. This is your addiction to methamphetamine.

I was the investigating officer of a serial armed robbery case which involved five robberies. After several weeks of showing photograph after photograph of gang members who matched the description of the suspects, I was able to identify five separate suspects and who were responsible for the robberies.

It would be ignorant on my part as an investigator to say witness intimidation does not occur in gang crimes. Are there cases of witness intimidation? Yes, of course, but law enforcement does a remarkable job keeping victims and witnesses safe considering the constraints enforced by the courts. In 18 years of law enforcement, I have never lost a victim or witness to anything remotely close to what would be considered witness intimidation.

During my serial robbery investigation, I had many victims who owned grocery stores, liquor stores, and meat markets, and who either did not watch much television or were not taken in by the very images society accepts via the 11 o'clock news.

The victims I dealt with during this investigation were people who took a stand and who also lived in the same community which bred the same people who would prey on them. The victims did not allow someone else to govern their lives, or let the gang members within the community to force them to live in fear. I usually had full cooperation from these people, who were of all races and nationalities. By the end of the investigation, I authored a multiple location search warrant. One location in particular was the residence of a female who aided in one of the robberies. She was very attractive and petite, the antithesis of the common profile. This girl was considered the ultimate **hyna**, or **hood rat** and every gang member in the neighborhood wanted her as their trophy. This girl was driven by the addiction that would change her life forever.

Deputies arrived for the early morning wake up call. The teams were strategically placed in areas of no detection, and when the early morning sun was about to illuminate the streets of the community, we were given the green light. When the dust settled and detentions were made, I along with my partner drove to each location. The search revealed gang paraphernalia, photographs, letters, and graffiti written on the walls. As I looked through the female's personal belongings, I came across the one piece of paper which would explain this girl's life, her choices and her ultimate demise. I found a poem, written by a young Indian girl who had fallen to the addiction of the devil. The poem is powerful in its accuracy and cuts deep with compassion:

"My Name Is Meth"
"I destroy homes, tear families apart, take your children, and that's just the start, I'm more costly than diamonds, more precious than gold, the sorrow I bring is a sight to be hold, if you need me I am easy to find, I live all around you, in your schools and in town, I live with the rich, I live with the poor, I'm down the street and maybe next door, I'm made in a lab but not like you think, I can be made under the kitchen sink, your child's closet or even in the woods, if this scares you to death, well then it certainly should, I have many names but there is one you know best, I am sure you have heard of me, my name is crystal meth, my power is awesome, try me you will see, but if you do, you may never break free, just try me once and I might let you go, but try me twice and I will own your soul, when I possess you, you will steal and lie, you do what you have to, just to get high, the crimes you commit for my narcotic charms, will be worth the pleasure you will feel in your arms, you will lie to your mother, you will steal from your dad, when you see their tears, you should feel sad, but you will forget your morals and how you were raised, I will be your conscience, I'll teach you my ways, I take kids from you parents and parents from kids, I turn people from God and friends, I take everything from you, your looks and your pride, I'll be with you, right by your side, you will give up everything, your family your home, your friends your income, then you will be alone, I will take and take, till you have nothing more to give, when I am finished with you, you will be lucky to live, if you try me be warned, this is not a game, if given a chance, I will drive you insane, I'll ravish your body, I will control your mind, I'll own you completely, your soul will be mine, the nightmares I'll give you while lying in bed, the voices you hear from inside your head, the sweats, the shakes, the visions you will see, I want you to know, those are all gifts from me, but then it's to late and you will know in your heart, that you are mine and we shall not part, you will regret that you tried me (They always do), but

you came to me, not I to you, you knew this would happen, many times you have been told, but you challenged my power, you chose to be bold, you could have said, "No", and then walked away, if you could live that day over now, what would you say? My power is awesome, as I told you before, I can take your life and make it so dim, so sore…
I'll be your master and you will be my slave, I'll even go with you when you go to your grave, now that you have met me, what will you do? Will you try me or not? It's all up to you.
I can show you more misery than words can tell,
come take my hand, let me lead you to hell."

I have attempted to find this author through every resource I am legally allowed to use, I have no idea how old she is, what her name is, where this was written or under what physical condition the author was in at the time she wrote this; I do not even know if she is alive. What I do know is that it is real and hits hard.

Gangs in society have the capability of not only taking over a city, but prey on those who are weak with addiction. I have been involved in narcotic-related investigations after the "wake up call". I interview the people who were arrested, but not for the actual street level sales of drugs from the house. I ask them why they allow this to occur in the very sanctuary they call **home**. Every time it is the same answer, "What else did you expect me to do Sloan, they just came in, and they needed a place to stay. I can't just kick them out."

Gang members use addiction as their friend. They sell drugs to weak individuals who cannot defend themselves physically, mentally or who have fallen for the devil which rages in their blood as a catalyst. However lucrative and powerful, the short-lived life of a drug dealer falls to the same paranoia created by his own product. The competitive life the gang member created for himself becomes his enemy. There is no trust, no allegiance and no honor in this lifestyle.

The drug dealer will employ the very person who will end up his enemy. They are usually younger gang members who are weaker in appearance, attempting to find their identity within the gang. These youngsters will easily fall prey to the so called "shot caller" of the neighborhood. This shot caller will ask members of the gang for protection, but protection from whom? Ultimately it is protection from the very people he refers to as his "home boys". This lifestyle of intimidation mixed with paranoia becomes the same enemy the drug dealer fights internally everyday. The seller is the user in most cases, and becomes, once again, the person who searches for the identity, acceptance, and status he craved before addiction.

Epiphany

The gang member finds out quickly after conviction exactly where he stands in the neighborhood. The letters stop coming; communication from his homeboys dwindles. The novelty of status wears off and time passes slowly during incarceration. To their surprise, no one checks on their family. Eventually the visits stop, and no money is placed in custody accounts. Typically, other gang members who are not incarcerated take advantage of opportunity by seeking attention and other favors from the incarcerated gang members girlfriend and/or wife. These favors range from live-in relationships to sexual gratification. Some learn faster than others, but all will eventually realize betrayal comes in many forms.

The gang member/drug dealer will do time in jail or confess to their sins in what would be an unforgivable act of betrayal for a gang. They know that if they confess to their sins and give up the jail time for the gang, their honor will be gone and thought to be a coward. They struggle with thoughts of years sitting alone in a 6x12 foot jail cell, but will keep their reputation intact. This is where they come face to face with the question; "is this lifestyle worth giving up my freedom"? This internal dialogue will mentally destroy the gang member and either choice will end in misery.

There is no honor in drugs and more often than not, the gang member talks. The shot caller has chosen the wrong soldier to take the fall. There is no resume or psychological exam to be dissected determining who he chooses to put in place as the patsy (fall guy). The shot caller selects the person who has vowed they would give their life to the neighborhood. The **Home Boy** often retains this vow until he is faced with lengthy jail time. The gang member usually asks for a deal and often begs to be out just long enough to see their child born, or to take care of their elderly mother or father. Desperation overthrows rational thinking as the gang member ponders the claustrophobia of incarceration. The normal every day aspects of life we take for granted are in jeopardy of being taken from the gang member—cold water, warm shower, the touch of a loved one, and free will. The feeling that the walls are actually closing in haunts the person who was put in charge of the everyday sales and fueling the abuser.

Even though methods of selling drugs have changed over the decades, the concept has remained the same. Cell phones, computers, burn out lines taken from unsuspecting victims of identity theft, have all changed how gang members utilize technology and have paved a way to a new and improved drug dealer. Identity theft has become a billion dollar industry, and the members of these gangs have capitalized on this. The abuser steals personal information, it is traded for drugs, and the drug dealer obtains goods and communication devices from the personal information stolen via the internet. The concept is still the same, dope houses, crack houses, flop pads, however referred too, will never change because of the demand for the devil. The weakness of the abuser and the inability to protect oneself from them as an addict will never go away. Those who continue to prey on the weak will ensure drugs will continue to remain available. The continued excuses of the abuser and addict who cry, "What else could I have done, what did you expect me to do, and I had no where else to go." I say to them, "You had a choice, you *always* have a choice."

In 1999 my life would change in terms of how I viewed society; it was also when I would become that "asshole cop". I pride myself on tactics and would never compromise myself or my partner's safety in any situation. We all have the flight or fight survival instinct. However, flight was never an option for me while working a gang infested area. I always fought and had never lost in my life. I accomplished everything I ever wanted to do. As a young man, sought a college scholarship and attended Long Beach State University playing baseball for the 49ers in 1983. I continued my success in baseball and fantasized of the chance to play baseball professionally. I accomplished this when in 1987, I was drafted by the Cincinnati Reds Baseball Organization, married the woman I loved since high school, and became a father to the son I adore. I had not allowed the word failure to enter my life and continued on into my next dream, law enforcement.

But on a particular day in 1999, I would fail. My ideology would be challenged, my attitude towards drugs, the people who abuse them, the people who sell them, my own safety, and my over-all view of the world would change forever. My partner, Mathew VanderHork, a brilliant street cop, who had the knack for finding the best arrests and the intellect of a Harvard professor, had an eye for crime. On this particular day, we heard a call go out to an assisting unit regarding a female who refused to leave a motel room. Both Matt and I knew the deputy who was given the call was busy on the other side of the city with another incident.

Knowing the motel and the reputation of the area being infested with gang members and drugs, in an area we referred to as a **cherry patch**, we decided to drive to the call, with the hopes of finding a good arrest, Upon arriving at the motel, I contacted the manager whom I had a very good rapport with. She had my phone number and if something did not look right, or if she felt illegal activity was being conducted at the business, she would contact me, and we would handle the problem without any incident.

On this particular day, however, she chose to make the call to the sheriff's station and ask for units to respond. She told me the cleaning lady was denied entry into a particular room, because a female who had stayed the night would not leave. Harmless enough we thought and the type of call that would normally take only a few minutes to remedy. Our mindset, because of past arrests, was that the female is probably wanted or in possession of illegal drugs.

I obtained the key to the room and walked up to the door. We looked into the window from a partially-closed curtain and could not see anyone. I unlocked the door with the key and swung it open so both Matt and I could have a visual of the entire room. I shouted into the room to announce our presence, and identified ourselves as police officers. No response. With our guns drawn we carefully and systematically entered, clearing every possible corner for a person hiding; under the bed, behind the door, etc… After clearing the room, we approached the door to the bathroom and peered into it.

I looked into the bathroom and saw the person who would change my life forever. I noticed a female, 25 or 26 years old, not a tiny girl, but definitely small in stature and weight. She was attractive, not really the type of female you would see in a motel like this. Her physical features were of a woman who had taken care of herself. You learn in this job that being able to effectively read people is crucial. You consider what are they wearing and what condition their clothes are in, how do they look physically, possible drug use, the care they take in their grooming, and other relevant questions. I noticed her hair was sandy blond and long, and appeared as if she had recently curled it. Her face was clear and pale, showing no signs of drug use or acne, scars, or marks routinely caused by drug use. Her shoes were white and clean as she was wearing a standard grey pull over sweat shirt that appeared to be clean.

As she sat on top of the covered toilet seat, I could see a look of concern, but nothing of paranoia. I greeted her and told her my name. The one thing about police work and staying alive means knowing where the suspect's hands are. Guns will not decide to kill you, but the hands which hold them will. I could see her hands the entire time as they lay on her thighs. I asked why she had not left yet and what was she hiding from. She addressed me with respect and spoke intelligently, showing no signs of a person who had the capability of doing what was about to happen. She explained she had been an outcast with her family and had been disowned by her father. She was truthful in telling us she had made some bad choices and had no where else to go. I gave her some options of what she could do, one of which was to be taken to an overnight shelter nearby. I explained to her she was trespassing and was not wanted at the motel-- trying to make her understand that she had to leave. Her personality never changed, she was solemn in her demeanor and her voice never fluctuated.

She agreed that she would like to have a ride to the shelter where she could gather her thoughts and figure out her next move. Unfortunately, her next choice would almost cost us our lives.

I stepped into the tiny bathroom and as I did this, the female's eyes widened, as if she had forgotten everything we had just talked about. Her half smile now became a face of rage, and the attractive, innocent female who had spoken to me so intelligently, would become a person of hate and anger. The female attempted to slam the door shut using her foot to close the door, which was unsuccessful due to the fact I weighed 210 pounds. I kicked open the half-closed door only to watch the female produce a blood curdling scream, a sound I will never forget, and she leaned her body backward towards the wall and retrieved a loaded .45 caliber semi-automatic handgun from under her sweatshirt. She lifted it to my chest, inches from my body.

My body blocked the view of my partner. As she lifted the weapon, I grabbed the barrel and yelled "Gun!" I jerked my body to the side, which happened to be where the bathtub was, in an effort to point the gun away from me and retrieve my weapon from my holster with my other hand.

The inevitable, which was burned into me with my training as a police officer had occurred; the instantaneous decision whether to live or die, to give up or fight, and to save the life of you or your fellow partner was swirling through my mind. Everything that had been taught to me regarding the effects of the human brain during a stressful situation was happening.

Although it happened in a split second, the suspect's actions seemed to be in slow motion. No sound could be heard, and during all of this, I instantly made the decision that I was going home that night. I was going to fight. I retrieved my gun from my holster, still holding on to the barrel of the girl's gun and attempting to point it away from my body. I noticed the gun was pointed directly at my partner, who was also retrieving his weapon in an attempt to return fire.

As I continued to raise my weapon to go underneath my right arm and fire a contact shot into the suspect, my body continued to fall vertically into the bath tub. I made a decision to point her weapon at my own leg, at the very least the wound will have a better chance of being non-fatal and where my partner stood would be out of the line of fire. I holstered my gun without securing it, and grabbed the barrel of the gun with both hands. While I did this, the female continued her shrieks of terror which were mostly deafened by the adrenaline gushing through my body. As I regained my balance the female pulled the trigger.

Continuous practice develops muscle memory where certain movements and actions almost became a natural act. To this day, I credit Matt VanderHorck with saving my life, because this was the day his continuous training would save both of us from being shot. Matt was able to grab the rear of the gun where the hammer falls into the firing pin, striking the primer to unleash the very bullet which was meant for either of us. The hammer ripped into his hand, cutting it severely, however the bullet was never fired from the gun.

Matt was able to take the gun from the female and secure it as we both took the female into custody by force. As the female laid on her stomach in hand cuffs, my hearing had finally returned and the screams the female were now more pronounced. She turned her head toward me and with a look of the devil, snarled, gasped and coughed, using every available breath to let us know she was not happy with the outcome. Screams only heard in a horror movie bellowed from this female who had gone instantly from a normal girl with some issues to a demonic entity, who would take the opportunity to destroy us if she could.

How did this happen? Two extremely sharp patrol deputies, tactically sound in every aspect of our job, and who could read fear, personality changes, and most of all, the signs of some one under the influence of drugs. What went wrong? The paramedics arrived to diagnose what would end up being a broken nose and ribs to the suspect. She was later interviewed by supervisors to determine if the force used was necessary and to question the suspect's mental state and the validity of her story.

The female spoke truthfully to our supervisor and explained she had been smoking methamphetamine for three straight days. Sleep depravation had taken over rational thinking, and the hallucinations methamphetamine had created over the past 72 hours had given her strength to fight and the mentality to kill her enemy; the enemy was ironically the two who had attempted to help her. She stated she had been in the motel room with members of a gang which plagued the very streets I patrolled every day, and even though she did not clearly admit it, we presumed she had exchanged sexual favors for the very drug which would ruin her life forever.

Today's vs. Yesterday's Gang Member

The mentality of today's gang member has mutated into a significantly more dangerous social deviant than past decades. The crimes have not changed, murder, robbery, rape, rival assaults, have all been a lifestyle and creed of the gang member. But the frequency, willingness, eagerness, and blatancy have become the aspect of the mentality that has only grown increasingly stronger.

I interviewed a gang member after he had been arrested for yet another senseless selfish act. He was older, pushing his mid-thirties or what would be considered "older" in the gang culture. I asked him what his take on today's gang member was and how was it different from when he was growing up in the late 80's. The gang member spoke candidly and made a statement which corroborated a thought process I had developed years before. Today's gang member has no honor and loyalty to the neighborhood or even to themselves (coincidentally characteristics of a gang member). He said when a problem had to be handled against either a rival gang or a member within their own gang; they took the initiative to handle the problem swiftly. Today's gang member, though still violent and untrustworthy, had to be under the influence in order to carry out the mission given to them by the shot caller. Or if they took it upon themselves in some retaliatory manner to impress other members to gain status, they had to fuel their minds with the drug that has mutated into an epidemic.

Why has today's gang member been fueled with chemical rage that has changed the mind and the soul to a killing machine with no regard for any human life? How could this mutation have occurred, and what was so different from 1970 to the present? Is it a coincidence that the mutation began when methamphetamine and crack Cocaine exploded on the streets?

In the hundreds of gang-related cases I have investigated, most of which were violent crimes. I noted during the capture of the suspects responsible for these crimes and ultimate interview of these suspects, most shared a common trait, an extreme addiction to drugs, mostly methamphetamine and rock cocaine. A blatant and uncaring attitude directed not only at themselves, but at society and innocent people as well. The suspect age group I was investigating was usually between 16 and 25. In the early 1980's rock cocaine arose throughout communities which changed the lives of millions and affected all social classes. Death, child abuse, addiction, and the break down of social classes were all affected by this one small entity that took the life of so many: Base cocaine also known as **rock or crack** cocaine. The abuse of Rock Cocaine went through the roof, and gang members of all races capitalized on this phenomenon to the profit of billions of dollars in financial gains nationwide.

Families were literally divided and destroyed and neighborhoods were overtaken by crack houses. One small drug, no bigger than a piece of salt rock, costing no more than 10 dollars and lasting only minutes, would become the focal point of distribution and the most important financial source of gangs throughout the world. The amount of female addicts was staggering as they lined up in droves and used whatever means necessary to obtain the next taste of the drug, prostitution, theft and sexual favors to the seller, commonly referred to as a **Strawberry**. However, because of the lack of protection used during these sexually enlightened times to keep from unwanted pregnancy, women of all races were finding themselves pregnant and with an even bigger problem, addiction which would last a lifetime, regardless of the human being growing inside of them.

These women, however far along in their pregnancies, continuously fueled their addiction creating in the end what was commonly referred to as a **Crack Baby**. This human life, who asked for nothing but love, would be born with an addiction which would last a lifetime, and be fueled only buy the very drug in which it was originally raised with. Having no chance in life, these children, who were born in overwhelming numbers reaching the millions, would suffer a life of desire for the very thing their brain would crave, until it is again fueled, but at ten times the potency.

The brain and central nervous system were being stimulated by the very chemical which they were plagued with while growing in their mother's womb. Susceptibility level increases and the brain never forgets. The level of addiction rises and the body grows weak with hunger once it has been exposed to the same feeling which has stayed dormant for so many years; until the one time it is exposed to the same stimulation it has unknowingly craved all those years. Many women have premature labor and deliver the baby too early. The baby born under these conditions suffer irreversible brain damage which is now showing up in teenagers with diagnosis such as: Attention Deficit Disorder, Dyslexia, hyperactivity and various mental disorders. These young people are being medicated by experts who never took the time to find out family history of addiction, which would once again fuel the subconscious addict with break-through medicines, all the while exposing the addict to a new temptation.

In the late 1980's and early 1990's, methamphetamine took the world by storm; at the street level it was considered a cheaper drug than cocaine or rock cocaine. Micro labs would pop up everywhere and in all levels of social classes. The people supplying this drug were utilizing household and industrial chemicals like hydrochloric acid, ephedrine, red phosphorous and regular solvents such as Freon or Coleman fuels to create what has been referred to as the devil. These chemicals create a deadly mixture, which if cooked correctly would create a super drug and over take the lives of the young and old. Communities would become prisons and people would live in fear of the people who abuse this mutated substance. Abuse of this drug would grow rapid, again, starting off as a party drug used to enlighten sexual experiences or just for the curious looking to get high. Women of all ages would flock to the drug, which was easily accessible and supplied by gang members looking for status. These gangsters within the drug community are referred to as a "**Baller**", which is an individual of financial and social stature, someone lying in wait for the next hood rat, strawberry, or woman looking for a way to fuel her addiction.

These women, while under the influence, and having no idea of the power of the drug they so desired fell into the trap of unwanted pregnancy. Once again, this pregnancy would bring a child into the world of addiction. The time frame and addiction in relation to today's gang member and the mutation which has occurred with the new mindset is something to consider.

The average age of gang members arrested for the most violent crimes are between the age of 16 and 25, born in the decade in which these drugs became main stream in gang communities. These children who were born with an addiction which had remained dormant for some 16, 17, and 18 years, waiting to be unleashed gets reborn into the world. Drug experimentation, unbeknownst to the curious user, mutates through the body and satisfies their subconscious urges. The vehicle pursuit on the news, the man driving a stolen tank down the freeway, the home invasion robbery, robbing the local clerk for just a few dollars, are committed by the person who has just been given a small taste of what they have subconsciously craved since the day of conception.

The human brain does not forget the stimulation which was fueled by an addicted mother. This rage can be unleashed by no more than one or two uses of the devil, and sends the user into an uncontrollable life of addiction and violent crime. It is a mentality of gang members which can be equated to that of which law enforcement was dealing with in the late 1970's and into the 1980's regarding PCP (phencyclidine). When PCP hit the mainstream with gang members, it literally changed tactics of law enforcement. This drug gave the abuser what was referred to as super human strength and paved the way to violent crimes.

Today's gang member is 100 times more dangerous and more likely to attack as the gang member several decades ago. They are committing these violent acts among the community without a thought or care - preying on anyone who they come across without any thoughts of repercussion or consequences. The mixture of mental disorders caused by the addiction to the very drug which governs their everyday actions; combined with an identity crisis and need for the acceptance, perpetuates their desire for status within the gang. This cycle can only be stopped in the early stages, before the inevitable occurs.

After Jerry Ortiz was murdered and the suspect was convicted a few select investigators drove Jerry's murderer to San Quentin State Prison to walk him down death row. We were going to introduce him to what life was going be like before he left this earth. During the drive to San Quentin, Jerry's murderer spoke candidly about his life. At times he was truthful and at other times, it was obvious he attempted to disassociate himself from pulling the trigger and playing God on that terrible day. As my partner Brandt House and I continued to converse with the criminal, it was evident we were speaking to someone who was delusional, brought on by the very drug that shaped his life and ultimately helped with the decision and choice that fateful day. The choice would pave the way to a life in a six by twelve foot cell, and personal imprisonment for eternity. He was cold, and possessed the death stare. Methamphetamine had taken over his mind, making it impossible for any rational thought or conversation.

He spoke as if he had some sort of relationship with Jerry, claiming past contacts; Jerry had treated him with respect and was well-known and respected within his gang. He also claimed he was not under the influence of meth at the time he shot Jerry, even though he never admitted to shooting him (He referred to it as the "incident").

He had a normal upbringing with Mexican national parents, who were hard-working and loved their children. He was never abused by his family, either verbally or physically. Although he did not have a normal gang member profile upbringing, methamphetamine changed everything and led to the decision that changed thousands of lives.

I am sure when he inhaled for the first time the hope which he so desperately sought was answered, giving him the strength, courage, and mentality of a leader. The drug entered his throat and ran through his lungs, ultimately seeking out his central nervous system and introducing itself to the brain. In one quick moment he made a decision to enter a world which would decide his fate in life; he chose to meet the devil head on and give his life to *crystal meth*.

We all have a choice.

Chapter eleven

The birth of a gang member and the effects of parental ignorance

From the late 1800's to the early 1900's, migration to the United States was staggering. For the most part, immigrants from Italy, Europe, and Ireland made their way to the states in hopes of a better life, better jobs, and a dream to be free from political oppression and economic disasters. These people who came to this country possessed a strong work ethic and traditional values regarding the roles of a spouse and the raising of children.

These immigrants were looking to start a new life for several reasons. One was to provide the quintessential aspects of life they were never able to have as a child. Another was to prove to themselves they could provide for their families a life filled with prosperity and hope. What was not considered, however, was that the United States was different from the traditions and values of where they came from. What was not considered was the United States was the land of opportunity for a reason. Immigrants were propelled into a new world, whose liberal views which allow us to express ourselves freely and without oppression come at a price. Citizens are allowed to make their own choices and pave the path to their own destiny. And choices have consequences.

Wide-spread immigration was not always the hard working family though. Criminals crossed our boarders and had an agenda. They were able to escape the barriers which held them back before, and take their enterprises to a country which continuously accepted the weak, the hungry, and those seeking a better life. However, a new life in a new country comes with new rules. Cultural differences on a small scale, in a small community, can initiate political and territorial enemies within the community.

Immigrants commonly segregate and live their lives under a blanket of their own culture. Seen in every race and every ethnicity; people were exposed to this way of life and it was popular for people to judge, solely on the area the people lived, their ancestry and religious beliefs. Citizens of these countries segregated themselves, not by color, physical appearance, race, social status or economical wealth; rather because of religious beliefs and the ancestral blood line in which they came from. This mindset transformed the immigrant communities into exactly what they fled; judged on where your family came from.

Cliques were formed and people of other descent were not allowed in areas because of their blood line. Children adopted the social structure and subculture which their parents refused to change. Children were not taught the value of freedom. This in turn, transformed the communities into the very same mentality which plagued their mother country, creating a criminal enterprise now "powered" by an open society. These criminals, ranging from petty thieves to the well known Mafia members, fed off of the political standing, religions, and ignorance of the middle class parent and child. This was sold to the community as for the "good of the neighborhood" and "for protection".

These parents took their same values, which in the sense of a working class were admirable. The parents failed in the fundamental foundation of what we were blessed with in our constitution. Neighborhoods were formed, cliques aligned, and a higher ranking structure was used as intimidation to the participants of these neighborhoods, thus forming what we know today as, the "birth of a gang member".

Parental ignorance is something I come across often in my line of work. The parents, both consciously and subconsciously, become the enabling foundation which creates the gang member.

Studies and criminal investigations reveal many gang members are created through generational gang ties. Children exposed to the gang lifestyle and become a direct link, falling victim to the constant exposure to gangs. This occurs due to desensitization of children in the household. It becomes normal to observe an older sibling using drugs, speaking gang dialect, for law enforcement to enter the residence via search warrants, knowledge of weapons within the household and many other factors. The decision to continue generational gang affiliation is difficult due to the constant pressure of conformity and the immaturity of youth.

This type of parent does not fall into the category of parental ignorance, they know exactly what is going on and have made the decision to ignore the issue. The parents have their own little kingdom which have possibly risen through the ranks of and exposed the children around them. They may not be gang members themselves, but like the buzz and energy that surrounds them. Some view the situation as a catalyst to the bond with the child in the only way they can. There are over 700,000 gang members in the United States and some experts place that number closer to a million.

The generational gang member's theory does not apply. Through all of my investigations, parental ignorance, be it consciously or inadvertent, has been the very foundation for the constant creation of the gang member. I have been involved with parents who, even if shown irrefutable evidence, refuse to admit to the status and activity level their child has within the structure of the gang. I have walked these parents through the child's bedroom. I even show the parent firsthand why their child, whether male or female, has been documented as a gang member. I show them writings, letters from people in state prison, music selection, and photographs. I show them pictures of their children flashing the gang sign which symbolizes the gang they claim. This information still however falls on deaf ears. To most parents, admitting to the child's gang status and membership would be admitting to failure as a parent. This same mentality becomes the foundation in the family, which ironically becomes the same reason the gang member was created: Hiding from the truth, trying to become the child's friend as opposed to being the child's parent and mentor.

The creation of the gang member does not fall into the traditional sense. From decades in the past, we stereotype these gang members as being formed from lower socioeconomic class, the "ghetto" as it has been referred to. Economic status or residential geographical areas one has to live in because of their financial situation is not an excuse for becoming the social deviant we fear. It is not an excuse to ignore our morals and values of what we believe to be socially correct, to raise our children and believe as to what is right and what is wrong. Our mindset should not change due to our economical and social status.

In so many investigations, the gang member is created by the very person who attempted to instill in their children, the same views towards this criminal lifestyle that they despise. But because of the unwillingness to accept that their children are human and capable of making poor life choices, they create a foundation within the home stating, "thou are not capable of doing wrong".

Each and every day we are subjected to countless acts of gang violence, the drive by shooting, the walk up shooting, the home invasion. We are constantly reminded of these acts of senseless violence through the media. And during these news clips, we all too often see the parent crying in the background, or whimpering as they are being interviewed. They tell stories of how the child was, a "good kid" who was liked by everyone in the neighborhood. They show a photograph of the deceased gang member when they were in fourth grade, even though the child who was killed was 17 years old. What happened to all of the photographs after fourth grade? Is it because the parent has come to the realization, they have helped to create a social deviant? Can they not admit to the truth of the failures as a parent to those around them who mourn the child's death?

The percentage of gang members who are generational is very low. Gang members come from all social boundaries, of all economical status. Parental ignorance is even more evident when there is no generational tie to any criminal street gang. Where did the parent think the child was, or what did they think the child was doing, when friends, obviously of gang affiliation, were coming over. The constant mobbing in the front yard, the drinking, the drug use, all the while turning a blind eye, helping to create the gang member and lifestyle the parents say they despise.

Parental ignorance and denial is the foundation which creates the gang member and continues to fuel the gangs who prey on communities. When it is brought to the attention of the parent, through school, law enforcement or other family members, taking the responsibility of what has happened should not be viewed as parental failure, but as any other parental issue which may arise during the parenting process. In many instances I have parents tell me they are fully aware of their child's participation in a gang. And all too often, I hear the same excuse, "I can't be here 24 hours a day, I have to work, I can't be held responsible for what is going on when I am not here."

We all have the choice of becoming a parent; however, I am not ignorant to what is referred to as unplanned pregnancy. I became a teenage parent and understand the pressures of attempting to balance a life with such an enormous responsibility. I am aware of the struggles of work, the overnight change in social life, and finding the time to become the parent we all knew we could be. It is a struggle to balance a foundation of right and wrong, knowing I could not be with my child 24 hours a day. The parent must teach self-reliance and independence and instill the confidence to say "no".

Children, through curiosity, chemical imbalance, peer pressure, substance abuse, and the need for acceptance can choose the wrong road in life. Parents can do a "perfect" job, do all the right things, make all the right decisions, and failure can still happen. However, what can not be condoned as a society and used for an excuse is, "children are not perfect and can fall prey to society's deviant behavior. They must be held accountable and suffer the consequences of poor decisions. We as parents, who have taken on the responsibility of parenting a child, have the obligation and responsibility to society and the child not to excuse the child's behavior and poor choices. Making excuses is only highlighting our own selfishness and inability to admit certain parental failures. Above all, we must not fall into the abyss of parental ignorance, which becomes the foundation for creation of the gang member.

There are certain physical attributes which can identify someone's lifestyle: clothing, hair style, choice of music, and areas they frequent. Also, street slangs and current, popular statements used by the child's peers. School attendance and their participation or lack of participation in activities, and pro-social or anti-social behavior are other indicators. Perceptions of a person's gang membership and affiliation by society are no different. Each generation of gang member is different in their clothing, hair, and musical styles. What does not change however is the fact the next generation is going to have a style and they are going to make it their own.

The clothing will change, hair styles will be different and the music will depict the lifestyle in which the gang represents. And as always, society through law enforcement and the people within the community will identify this and perceive it as criminal.

We will categorize the people who are attempting to identify themselves through this current style as a criminal group. We have to ask ourselves, if there is a perception of specific styles being of a criminal subculture; who is purchasing the items which represent the person as part of this criminal group? Parents must realize it is okay and well within their rights, in fact, it's their responsibility to say, "**no**." Too many guardians dismiss the "gangsta" look as "in style" and pay for the items. Who is allowing these youngsters to live in their houses, eat their food, and engage in criminal actions? This is only accomplished through the parent, who lies, harbors, and encourages the child consciously or subconsciously by setting the foundation known as parental ignorance. They excuse negative behavior and encourage creation of the gang member by doing nothing to stop it.

Gangsta rap

Parental ignorance is rampant in this area. Many minimize the lifestyle, message and lyrics as a "phase all young people go through." The media glamorizes these performers, ultimately assisting in the desensitization of America with its anti-societal diatribe and degradation of women. Below are lyrics from one of these songs:

got my black shirt on
I got my black gloves on
I got my ski mask on
This shit's been too long

I got my twelve gauge sawed off
I got my headlights turned off
I'm 'bout to bust some shots off
I'm 'bout to dust some cops off

Cop killer, better you than me
Cop killer, fuck police brutality
Cop killer, I know your family's grievin'
Cop killer, but tonight we get even

I got my brain on hype
Tonight'll be your night
I got this long-assed knife
And your neck looks just right

My adrenaline's pumpin'
I got my stereo bumpin'
I'm 'bout to kill me somethin'
A pig stopped me for nuthin'

Cop killer, better you than me
Cop killer, fuck police brutality
Cop killer, I know your mama's grievin'
(Fuck her)
Cop killer, but tonight we get even

Cop killer, better you than me
I'm a cop killer, fuck police brutality
Cop killer, I know your family's grievin'
(Fuck 'em)
Cop killer, but tonight we get even

Cop killer, cop killer, cop killer, cop killer
Cop killer, what you're gonna be when you grown up?
Cop killer, good choice, cop killer
I'm a muthafuckin' cop killer

Cop killer, better you than me
Cop killer, fuck police brutality
Cop killer, I know your mama's grievin'
Cop killer, but tonight we get even

You will never hear a grieving parent, after their child was killed in yet another senseless act of violence, who will say, "My child was killed because they were a gang member."

We all have a choice.

Chapter twelve

Solving crime

Signs and Symbols: the true meaning behind them and how they help the investigator.

I have testified as an expert on gangs throughout the court system. There is a basic format to the line of questioning for a gang expert. The questioning can change from time to time and certain aspects or questions can change depending on the district attorney or county you are testifying in. The one question that is always asked regardless of boundaries or district attorney is, "Detective, are there any common signs or symbols that identify the gang?"

The individualism that derives through **Acceptance, Recognition, and Status** can only be symbolized by how the gang member is recognized. But the meaning is much more than what has been sensationalized by television, movies, and written biographies. The symbolization one uses to identify themselves as an individual ,as well as a gang, takes on more than just the recognition one achieves from graffiti or a hand gesture known as, **being banged** on or **flashing**. To take it a step further, signs, symbols, and monikers signify a time line a gang member inevitably will travel as they seek ranking, acceptance, recognition and status. These signs, symbols, hand gestures, and writings become the symbol of the life they have chosen.

The importance of the individual tag of graffiti, gang sign, moniker and paraphernalia which symbolizes the individual as well as the neighborhood never sways. Almost considered ritual or gospel, the signs and symbols which a gang member or gang uses to romanticize themselves in an effort to be accepted and recognized. Society views them as vulgar and of a lower social class; the gangsters see it as just the opposite, a statement to show they have been accepted into an elite group.

Over the years, gang slang terms have changed in their content and meaning, and with every passing generation of up-and-coming gang members, the evolution of styles and clothing also change.

Fame

The transformation of the individual demonstrates to those who, in the gang member's eyes can offer an identity and acceptance into a world they believe is above everyone else. His efforts are validated by the individual transformation from searching to acceptance. They have been given the right, by the very gang which brought him or her to fame. The individual is given a name, which he or she will be known as for the rest of their life. They will look at themselves as an elitist or special. They will be given the chance to **claim** a new world which allows them to do what they want and take what they want. If cornered by rivals or law enforcement, they will be given the protection they have searched for, not understanding protection is only needed by those who have been accepted into a world which constantly needs protection.

Once accepted into a neighborhood, it is not just a desire to show society who they are, it is a need. It becomes an obsession and addiction to constantly let the neighborhood which raised and accepted the gangster, as well as the rivals who threaten the individual and demand to know "who they claim"..

The individual not only wants their face to be seen, but their name to be recognized. Needing others to know their name, whether it is displayed on a wall, etched into a business glass window, scratched into an elevator door, or written on a toilet seat: they want everyone to know they have been accepted into a criminal organization in which only very few are permitted entry. The fear the gangster mistakes for respect overflows into the community and brings a new sense of awe, in which the gang member feeds. The community ultimately accepts it as a part of daily life. Most will have no affiliation to the neighborhood gang which claims the territory as their own, but will stay out of the way. The community is affected socially, because society has labeled the neighborhood to be a lower class of people, when in actuality the number of people creating this fear is a very small percentage of the total population. The individuals who choose to tag the very name which symbolizes their identity and promote the gang, takes advantage of people through fear and intimidation. Members of a community are to look the other way and mind their own business. After all, in the gang member's mind, criminal activity doesn't concern or have anything to do with them.

The fear in a community occurs because they believe severe repercussions will come to those who interfere. They are held prisoner in a community that is littered with writings and graffiti. The gang sprays their names in the shadows behind fences, residential walls, and defaces the local business owner's livelihood. Symbols constantly remind the members of the community of their sheep-role in society. To make the members of society understand that to live in that area is to accept the area. They encourage acceptance in a number of ways: graffiti, stare-down, vandalism and burglary. Acceptance by citizens come at a price, and the price is a life of acknowledgment that even though they are strong in numbers and possess the ability to say "no more", they mind their own business. They will say the contrary, but the truth is they are imprisoned in their own homes. People of the community accept the writings sprayed on their own houses as the price they pay to stay safe; choosing the path of least resistance is easier in the short term, but will cost much more in the long term.

Solving Crime with graffiti and signs/symbols

Signs, symbols and gang monikers are invaluable to police officers and investigators and become the forefront to any investigation; they become as important to an investigation as the smoking gun or the bloody glove. Understanding the area in which a police officer or detective is investigating brings an incredible amount of intelligence and importance to solving a crime. Having knowledge of the current trends in graffiti of the neighborhood is vital to any gang detective. It tells a story of current members and past convictions and who they are at war with, which can be the difference between solving a crime or closing a case unsolved. For example: a younger generation gang member may take on the gang name of an older generation gang member, so knowledge of gang member names could indicate which gang committed a certain crime.

Gang names are given for numerous reasons, such as the death, be it criminal or natural of an older generation gang member, the recent incarceration and conviction of a fellow gang member or showing respect to a family member or older generation gang member who wore the moniker with pride. These younger generation gang members take these names with a sense of history and tradition, because they are given the opportunity to continue a legacy for the future generation. These names can only be used with permission and no gang member may ever take it upon themselves to further their recognition and status without consent. Self proclamation or self-naming is common, but only on original names and monikers.

These names and monikers are taken in this context:

"Lil Bird"
"Lil Thumper"
"Baby Rey"
"Stocky II"
"Lil Evil"

"Guns II"
"Sniper 2"
"Baby Gloves"
"Lil BooBoo"

Possessing this knowledge as an investigator or police officer can enable you to take control of an investigation and have an idea of who you are looking for and/or who is responsible for a recent crime wave. It is not difficult to find gang members who cooperate with the police and give up the moniker of a gang member who is responsible for recent crimes. It is common for them to only be able to identify the suspect by their gang name or moniker because that is all they have ever heard. Younger generation gang members who were exposed to older generation members by fathers, mothers, and brothers will not know the birth name of its founders.

First rule in the gang life is "don't ask questions". You do not take the time to sit down and have a conversation about an individual's social or financial status, current affairs, or what their favorite hobbies are. Once the person is introduced as such, that is who they are. Unless someone offers an actual name or the individuals grew up together in school, the person who identifies themselves as "Sniper" is only known as "Sniper." The identity of the person can be non-existent and is of no concern to the individuals around them. The name or moniker which has been assigned to the gang member is an identity reborn and is a name carried with honor. The name symbolizes the world in which the gang member has chosen and it is abundantly clear it is the job of the investigator to be able to recognize this trend. The detective will investigate past incidents, court cases, deaths, and school incidents, in order to recognize and determine why they took the name.

These signs, names, and monikers are not the only identifiable aspects created by gang members. Limiting yourself to only one aspect of identity and not acknowledging that graffiti exists is ignorant and can mean solving or not solving the case. Gang paraphernalia, symbols, animated characters, music, clothing styles, and tattoos are all identifiable aspects of an individual's affiliation and gang identity. In the early 80's, gangs identified from back east such as the "Latin Kings" of Chicago, made no effort to hide their identity. Flashy colors and clothes which are worn to symbolize their affiliation, status, and gang, continue to be utilized to this day. These aspects of gang paraphernalia can be as easily hidden from law enforcement and parents as a color. Since the dawning of the Crips and Bloods black gangs in the 70's, mainly centralized out of the south central areas of Los Angeles, we have been exposed to the colors of blue and red. As the evolution of gangs has turned and the trends are set by future gang members we must be aware that times change.

In 2000, I noticed a trend within a black gang which was what I considered an evolution to what had been started by the all too well known "Crip/Blood mentality," a simple color change. These black gang members did not identify with Crip or Blood, blue or red, they identified as an individual even though they engaged in the same criminal behavior as a group, mentioned in the penal code section of 186.22. These gang members took the mentality of sex and money as a basis to what they believed identified themselves as a gang. It was about the individual, not the gang or the neighborhood. There was no territory, and with the exception of local flier parties being broken up police would rarely find a group mobbing outside intimidating or creating fear in the community. It was about making as much money as possible, by selling drugs, committing burglary and commercial theft, and more importantly sexually exploiting as many young women as possible.

Still the same mentality: acceptance, recognition and status, validated by the writings on the wall, but members of this criminal organization refused to identify themselves as a Crip or Blood. Instead they harbored a high level of animosity towards anyone who identified with the Crip or Blood criminal street gangs. This group attempted to maintain individuality, but adopted the color green which ultimately created like-mindedness. Color changes of green sprung up all over the local schools. Parents suffering from parental ignorance refused to believe their children were in a gang, because the traditional aspects of gang identification were not present.

Returning to the challenge of parental efficacy, it is imperative parents do not excuse or minimize the teenager's new look with statements such as, "That is the style now." Or "We had our look, this is theirs." Or, "He's just going through a phase." He will grow out of it." A parent need not and should not be a "friend". They should do everything within their power to keep young people away from the slippery slope of societal deviancy. Parents need to educate themselves and take away their childrens "gangsta rap", throw away the baggy pants and long shorts, keep the kids structured and busy.

A full circle of tradition had evolved. What was considered flashy in the 80's has been forgotten and reborn to again identify this particular group of individuals. Traditional gang names were being replaced with names like "Sexy Banana" **(True name of a serial robbery suspect I investigated in 2004, responsible for ten armed robberies)**. This particular trend of signs and symbols was recognized immediately by members of law enforcement. The information was disseminated to the local schools, communities, and to outside law enforcement and used as an identifiable tool in the solving of numerous violent crimes.

Flashing gang signs, or as referred to on the streets as **Banging on someone**, is one of the most common symbols used by gang members to identify themselves as an individual, as well as promoting their gang. This ritual is a basis for acknowledgment and recognition and is used in all fashions of intimidation. Mostly, two members who are possibly of rival gangs will use their fingers to simulate an abbreviation which identifies their particular gang. They do this in an effort to promote, intimidate and show their allegiance to their particular criminal street gang. This ritual is used by all gangs regardless of the race and can only be used by a validated member. Again, privileges such as **Banging on someone** have to be earned by the individual and can only be accomplished once they have been accepted and recognized as a member. I have been involved in utilizing the gang enhancement set forth by state legislation and have been able to identify these incidents as gang crimes and the gangs involved simply by what happened minutes before the incident.

Witness statements made during interviews have verified what provoked the crime, who had provoked it, and who was responsible, simply because the suspect/victim could not resist the temptation of symbolizing their gang status and affiliation by a symbolic hand gesture which identified themselves as a gang member. Witnesses will actually mimic the hand sign once asked to do so by myself or the district attorney during an interview.

We all have a choice.

Chapter thirteen

Legislation and court procedures

A Remedy to Gangs: steps within the District Attorney's Office and Law Enforcement to battle the epidemic.

"Criminal Street Gang" is defined as any ongoing organization, association, or group of three or more persons, whether formal or informal, having a common name or common sign and who's members individually or collectively engage in or have engaged in a pattern of criminal gang activity. (penal code section 186.22 subsection F)

In 1988, after years of gang related murders plagued the streets of the United States, one of the most well needed judicial laws was implemented. The S.T.E.P. Act (STREET TERRORISM ENFORCEMENT AND PREVENTION ACT) was initiated and literally changed the way gang crimes were prosecuted by the District Attorneys office. Under Penal Code section 186.21, the S.T.E.P. Act reads as follows:

The Legislature hereby finds and declares that it is the right of every person, regardless of race, color, creed, religion, national origin, gender, age, sexual orientation, or handicap, to be secure and protected from fear, intimidation, and physical harm caused by the activities of violent groups and individuals.

It is not the intent of this chapter to interfere with the exercise of the constitutionally protected rights of freedom of expression and association. The legislature hereby recognizes the constitutional right of every citizen to harbor and express beliefs of any lawful subject whatsoever, to lawfully associate with others who share similar beliefs, to petition lawfully constituted authority for redress or perceived grievances, and to participate in the electoral process.

The legislature, however, further finds that a state of crisis which has been caused by violent street gangs whose members threaten, terrorize, and commit a multitude of crimes against the peaceful citizens of their neighborhoods. These activities, both individually and collectively, present a clear and present danger to public order and safety and are not constitutionally protected.

In this same section, at the time the law was written, legislature was documenting 328 gang related murders in Los Angeles County alone in 1986. Further, statistics showed the increase in gang murders up 80 percent in 1987. Today, in Los Angeles County, which is utilized as a microcosm of the entire country, we have over 1,200 documented criminal street gangs. Gang murders in 2005 made up almost 35 percent of all murders.

As of today, the laws under penal code section 186.22 have been changed and been revised significantly. The "dirty 30," as it was referred to as by law enforcement and deputy district attorneys, has revamped the sections under this same penal code since its inception. The "dirty 30" are 30 different crimes which have been shown to be committed by gang members on a regular basis, and can be tried in a court of law as a gang crime. Presently there are 33 crimes under this section (186.22 subsections (e)) which allow the district attorney's office to enhance as a gang crime as well as the sentence enhancement of the individual being charged. This allows the district attorney's office to additionally charge the individual with what is considered a gang enhancement, which can substantially raise the bail and sentence to any of the 33 listed gang crimes in most states.

As an example, penal code section 182, conspiracy can carry a state prison sentence in the same manner and to the same extent as is provided for the punishment of that felony in which the suspects were conspiring to commit. This sentence is going to be determined by past criminal history and prior prison terms of the individual. However, this same conviction with a gang enhancement has the capability of sentencing the individual to life in prison. This tool has enabled the district attorney's office to maintain a continuous pattern of long-term prison sentences on gang members which enables law enforcement to maintain order in areas plagued with generational gang activity. These neighborhoods have dramatically increased in quality of life--living now without fear and intimidation.

In the past these crimes would have resulted in a light sentence in the criminal gang world, but has now evolved into mandatory sentencing which a judge can not over rule. This keeps the gang member incarcerated for a substantial amount of time as prior sentencing guidelines limited the bargaining power from the district attorney's office, when it came to plea negotiations or sentencing. Because the gang enhancement provides mandatory sentencing a gang member cannot sit and wait for a typical 16 month sentence and with a mandatory state law of "half time" rule, with good time and work time the gang member would do a total of 8 months in prison. Hardly a sentence for a career criminal, or much of a deterrent for the gang member to cease the lifestyle they have chosen. Now, with an aggressive district attorney who is knowledgeable of current gang laws, the state is now in a position to either plea a long sentence, or the defendant risks a life sentence if found guilty.

I have been involved in some of the most noteworthy and horrific investigations involving gang members. Serial robberies, kidnapping, attempted murder, and murder, all for the benefit of, in association with, and at the direction of the gang. It was because of these laws that I along with the district attorney's office was able to convict those responsible. With a gang allegation and life sentence looming, it is a regular occurrence for a defense attorney to come to us and ask for an offer in the 20-year category.

We have had defense attorney's ask for offers and when the district attorney asks, "Well, what are you looking for?" The answer is usually, "anything but life." The pendulum has swung to the side of the citizen, and is creating a quality of life worth living in areas that continue to be plagued by the monster. These 33 crimes continuously committed by gangs, which have haunted communities for decades and recognized by the district attorney's office as destroying lives and cities, has set precedence for the future. We now approach these incidents with a rejuvenated vigor knowing prosecution is inevitable.

These 33 gang crimes, listed under this section within the 186.22 P.C. are as follows:
(1). Assault with a deadly weapon, either force or by weapon, 245 P.C.
(2). Robbery, 211P.C.
(3). Homicide or unlawful Manslaughter, 187P.C.
(4). The sale, transportation, possession for sale, manufacture, offer for sale, offer to manufacture any controlled substances as defined in 11054 through 11058 of the Health And Safety Code.
(5). Shooting at an inhabited dwelling or occupied motor vehicle, 246P.C.
(6). Discharging or permitting the discharge of a firearm from a motor vehicle as defined in 12034P.C.
(7). Arson, 450.P.C. sections.
(8). The intimidation of witnesses and victims, 136.1P.C.
(9). Grand Theft, 487 P.C.
(10). Grand Theft of any firearm, vehicle, trailer or vessel.
(11). Burglary, 459 P.C.
(12). Rape, 261 P.C.
(13). Looting, 463 P.C.
(14). Money Laundering, 186.10 P.C.
(15). Kidnapping, 207 P.C.
(16). Mayhem, 203 P.C.
(17). Aggravated Mayhem, 205 P.C.
(18). Torture, 206 P.C.
(19). Felony Extortion, 518 and 520 P.C.

(20). Felony Vandalism, 594 P.C.
(21). Carjacking, 215 P.C.
(22). The sale, delivery or transfer of a firearm, 12072 P.C.
(23). Possession of a pistol, revolver, or other capable of being concealed upon a person, 12101 P.C.
(24). Threats to commit crimes resulting in death or great bodily injury 422 P.C.
(25). Theft and unlawful taking or driving of a vehicle, 10851 V.C.
(26). Felony theft of an access card or account information.
(27). Counterfeiting, designing, using, attempting to use an access card, 484f P.C.
(28). Felony fraudulent use of an access card or account information, 484g P.C.
(29). Unlawful use of personal identifying information to obtain credit, goods, services, or medical information, 530.5 P.C.
(30). Wrongfully obtaining Department Of Motor Vehicle documentation, 529.7 P.C.
(31). Prohibited possession of a firearm, 12021 P.C.
(32). Carrying a concealed firearm, 12025 P.C.
(33). Carrying a loaded firearm, 12031 P.C.

In 1979, the Los Angeles District Attorney's Office implemented what would become at present time, one of the most aggressive aspects at fighting gang crimes in Los Angeles County. The HARD CORE GANG UNIT would be born and become the most aggressive aspect at fighting gangs in Los Angeles County. Some of the brightest, most aggressive, and talented deputy district attorneys would be recruited for the position: veterans who are some of the hardest working individuals at the district attorney's office. They then knew the hours would be long, the work overwhelming, but because of a passion for their work, tenacity at their profession and desire to give quality of life to the people who needed it most, they accepted the position. They were transformed into the work horses within the district attorney's office and would become the focal point at what is considered a very political environment. Many of these

D.A's will attain the honor of judge, and it is well-deserved. These individuals take on an impossible task, and because of their moralistic views towards the quality of life in which we all should be given the opportunity to live in at the highest level, these individuals give up more than most to constantly pursue the unrelenting violent gang crimes.

Law enforcement and the district attorney's office often state, "a gang murder is the easiest to solve, but the hardest to prosecute." As written before, the obstacles in a successful prosecution of a violent gang case can be daunting. However, these individuals who take on the task of the impossible somehow make it work.

In November of 2005, I was fortunate enough to meet a man who would become a personal friend of mine. His name is Mike Enomoto, a Deputy District Attorney with the Los Angeles County District Attorney's Office who was working Hard Core Gangs. Mike was born of Japanese descent and raised with a solid foundation. He changed the mentality of the Hard Core Gang Unit with his aggressive prosecution of gang members. He possesses extensive knowledge of the penal code, policies within the district attorney's office, and a non-stop work ethic. Mike is feared by defense attorneys because of his professionalism, integrity, and brilliance. He is one of the most respected employees at the Los Angeles County District Attorney's Office and has been summoned by the state legislature to implement new legislation to curb the on-going gang problem. Mike has testified in front of the State Assembly and Senate, and was instrumental in the passing of new laws governing parental responsibility for their children. These laws made it so that parents are now held accountable for the actions of their children that fall into the "first time offender" category. He is truly one of the best public speakers in his field and sought-out by peers for his advice and mentoring on a daily basis.

Relationships between law enforcement and the district attorney's office are vital when it comes to successful prosecution. If there is a breakdown in communication between the two, the end result can be catastrophic. Respect between the prosecutor and the investigator has to be almost at the personal level in order to get through what can be an overwhelming amount of work and preparation. The investigator can not think their job is finished when they have successfully filed a case against a gang member. In fact, the work has just started. Evidence discovery motions, evidence suppression motions, witness and victim relationships, and investigation follow up are just a few aspects of what the DA faces in a single case. Imagine doing this with approximately 65 to 70 cases a year. Relationships within law enforcement and the district attorney's office will be the difference between success and failure. My partner and I have been fortunate to have worked with the best of the best regarding district attorneys. Failure is not an option and plea bargain does not exist in our world. We approach every case as if it is going to go to trial and the preparation has to be at the highest level.

This can only be accomplished by a full understanding and respect for the deputy district attorney and the investigator. In our line of work there is no such thing as getting caught up. It is a never ending turnstile and it takes all you have to stay above water without drowning in your own creation. As an investigator I have never said no to a request made by the district attorney regarding any aspect of any case, nor would I ever. Failing to follow through would be further victimizing the community, witnesses and victims all over again. Relationships between the DA's office and Law Enforcement have to be on equal ground, and personality conflicts should be handled swiftly with no room for egos. Both sides work together and listen to each other in order to accomplish the ultimate goal of bringing the gang member to justice.

I have a tremendous amount of respect for Mike Enomoto because he understands the urgency of what we do and has an equal amount of respect for law enforcement. Mike knows the importance of building relationships within the law enforcement community and actually works the streets as a reserve police officer with a neighboring agency. He has taken the police officer/DA relationship to the next level and understands the ultimate goal. I can not express enough to new investigators, police officers, and students looking into a Law Enforcement as a career how important it is to develop professional relationships. As for Mike Enomoto, I have a very strong feeling I will some day be addressing him as "Your Honor".

Lawyers & Court

I was once asked by the district attorney's office to testify as an expert in an attempt-murder trial regarding a gang I was very familiar with. Testifying as an expert can be tedious and time consuming. It often depends on whether the defense attorney was retained as private counsel, meaning, have they been hired by the defendant or the defendant's family as a private attorney. If anyone in the family works for the court system they will have an access to the best attorneys.

One of the things I find so interesting about our court system is the different personalities of the defense attorneys. You will find all types, some who are professional and personable, some who are believers, and some just there for a paycheck. There are a few who do the job because they agree with the system and believe everyone is entitled to fair representation. There is also a small percentage of crusaders; attorneys who truly believe everyone in law enforcement is involved in a complete conspiracy, who believe the client first, refute the evidence presented and will not take into consideration the source of information. Their personal egos block their client's best interest and control of the defendant is non existent. These wayward and naive professionals never come to the realization that they have fallen prey to the same manipulation techniques the career criminal utilizes on their victims every day.

On this particular case, I testified to my reasons why a gang member continues their criminal life and the ultimate goal a gang member seeks. The defense attorney questioned me on cross-examination after the district attorney had finished direct questions. The defense attorney had focused in on several aspects of my testimony. He ended with a line of questions in an attempt to disprove my findings of **Acceptance**, **Recognition** and **Status** as related to the rise of rank and sociological levels within the structure of the gang by his client.

The attorney asks, "Detective Sloan, would it be safe to say, that the theories you touched on can fall under the category of what any person wants in life?" I assured the defense attorney my findings were not theory, "No" I stated. The attorney followed up with, "Well, doesn't everyone want to be accepted in a group, doesn't everyone want to be recognized by their friends, peers and employers, and doesn't everyone want to be seen in some sort of status symbol by either their family or maybe their co-workers?" "Detective Sloan, don't you want to be looked upon with recognition and status as a person the Los Angeles County Sheriff's Department can trust in a crisis situation, or say, maybe to train new deputies?" I answered, "Yes sir, but the only difference between me and your client is I wouldn't attempt to kill someone to seek acceptance, recognition and status."

"No further questions," and as the defense attorney walked back to the table towards his client, he smirked at me as if to say, 'I walked right into that one'.

We all have a choice.

Chapter fourteen

The answer to destroying gangs

How do we fix what is inevitable?

We have allowed gangs to form into an acceptable subculture which prey on not only the weak, but the strong. How do we actually solve a problem which has taken hold of our lives domestically, socially, and cost us literally billions in law enforcement resources, failed programs and the most important thing imaginable, the gift of life?

I sat down with a man I have admired and respected ever since the day I first walked into his courtroom, Judge Leland Tipton. He is an extremely brilliant man whose knowledge of the law is second to none. His courtroom demeanor is that of a true professional and his belief in the system and the law is apparent to all.

He had a very simple approach to the law; each case would be judged solely by the evidence. I understand this sounds elementary almost to the point of asking: "how else would he approach his position?" It was more than that with Judge Tipton. I never once observed him alter his decorum or show any display of emotion toward any party. In all cases, Judge Tipton felt it was his duty as a magistrate to look at all facts without prejudice. He was ethical and always the true professional. One day while having him read and approve yet another search and arrest warrant, we had a conversation that was very dear to my heart.

What causes gangs and what is the answer to eradicating them?

On this particular day, the court room calendar was light and we had a few minutes. We spoke about his court case load and his views regarding society and gang life. Judge Tipton stopped for a brief moment, looked at me and said "We have got to break the cycle." A simple, but profound answer to what we now call normal, from someone who has seen it all, heard it all, and tried an untold number of gang cases. The statement went beyond the boundaries of one concept or idea. He was right, it's not enough to attack singular components of the issue; we need to break the cycle of generational gang members, culture, socioeconomic situations and glamorization of the gangster life.

I have expressed my views throughout this book of my non-belief of generational gang members, or being the product of the environment since we all have a choice. However, as stated earlier in the book; it would be irresponsible not to acknowledge the desensitization the generational gang member traverses through due to the exposure to the gang lifestyle. The holistic approach uttered by Judge Tipton, meant so much more.

We as a society need to take responsibility for what we have allowed to exist for so long. Lawmakers and law enforcement have attempted to stop the bleeding of society by placing only a band aid on it. We accept this and continue to bandage a wound that will never heal. Society has evolved into the highest standard of living in history, but if we continue to allow the animal to feed, letting the animal to get stronger, bigger, and take over.

We have exposed gangs through television, movies and music. We have at times praised it and shown it as an actual lifestyle through what we believe to be good television and entertainment. Sensationalism of a certain group, whether positive or negative, can fuel an individual because we have to understand what the individual's motive is for this lifestyle choice. In this case, acceptance, recognition, and status sparks the gang member who claims it is actually for a certain group, area and neighborhood, when in the end, it is for personal gain. Finding an attraction to this life style is a validation in the eyes of the person who obsesses for this acceptance.

We as a social civil society speak of this lifestyle in a collective group as menacing, threatening, monstrous, socially unacceptable, and wrong, while in the same breath we tell our families, "not to get involved" and "it's not my problem." Unfortunately, this is our problem. In one breath we weep for the innocent victim and damn the people involved. With the next breath, only due to complete parental ignorance, we condone the adulation celebrities espousing the gang lifestyle, accept the life they choose, and continue to allow the gang to prey as we fuel them with excuses. Through parental ignorance we oppose legislature to make the parent responsible for their children's actions, while they continue a never ending cycle of disobedience. Proper parental efficacy would collapse the stronghold of every gang in America; unfortunately we will continue to hear all too often, "what did you want me to do? I can't watch them every minute of the day"

The parent who allows the child to leave without warning and continues to supply excuses and alibis, refusing to challenge poor choices made by their child will be visiting them in prison and/or planning their funeral. They excuse the child's sins by refusing to accept their own parental failures. They place the daily decisions in the child's hands, claiming: "If I did it, then they can do it." There will be no acceptance even after death, only blame for law enforcement for failing to protect their baby.

I agree with the 1st amendment, freedom of expression and freedom of speech, culture, family, and tradition. I also believe in quality of life and if society continues to allow gang members to hide behind the constitution there will be no quality of life. I became a deputy sheriff for one reason and one reason only, to protect those who could not protect themselves. If we as a society want to truly take hold of this problem, than it is time we break the cycle. All of us must take responsibility for a problem that began decades ago and has now for the most part become a low income geographical problem. We allowed this to occur and perpetuate, in the end poured billions of dollars into resources when the answer was in front of us the entire time.

Let's break the cycle by holding each individual accountable for their actions, and make the gang members understand that their actions will not be tolerated. Show them this lifestyle choice is going to be extremely detrimental to their future.

As law enforcement agencies, we need to work directly with the media, not only at the levels of local news, but create educational workshops with movie and film industries to show the affects of sensationalism and how it can fuel the gang member's validation. They excuse the gang lifestyle and turn thugs into charismatic sex symbols. In open forums, society speaks disparagingly of the lifestyle, but also excuses it by listening to the manipulation the monster provides as validation for their actions. This same society makes a hero out of a murderer that later wrote a children's book.

We have to stop looking at this lifestyle as a subculture that only affects those geographic areas which have been deemed of lower economical status, and understand that just like drug and alcohol abuse, gang life affects every social economical class we have validated as acceptable. We must take note that constant sensationalism and intrigue by society fuels the gang, and will only raise the level of fondness of the gang lifestyle the individual continues to choose.

We all have a choice.

Chapter fifteen

Anti-corruption legislation

What do state law makers and legislation need to do? They should re-evaluate and go to the source of the problem and to the line of experts for the answers. Cities and counties throughout the United States have introduced various sanctions and injunctions, targeting specific gangs who have proven to be criminal enterprises and the source of the area's decline. These injunctions have proven very successful and pave the way for the community's recovery and success. Within these gang injunctions, provisions and conditions are placed upon the gang and the members. The conditions make life so uncomfortable that there are only two choices the gang member can make. Stay in the area and change their lifestyle, or move to avoid constant arrest for violating the conditions of which the injunction has sanctioned.

In 2005, I was chosen as one of five investigators to lead a federal investigation against a criminal street gang which had plagued a city for decades. At the end of this investigation, the United States Attorney General announced the largest federal gang investigation in United States history had ended with over two hundred gang members and affiliates being indicted. The gang injunction I have previously spoke of facilitated by Deputy District Attorney Deane Castorina was implemented. The gang injunction was signed by a civil judge in downtown Los Angeles in 2007 with lifetime conditions. Since the induction of this lifetime gang injunction, violent crimes ranging from murder, robbery, assaults, and residential burglaries have dropped an unprecedented 70% from the previous two years. These statistics are undisputed and an example of what a gang injunction can do if implemented.

A state wide gang injunction is not unrealistic nor is it unconstitutional. Identifying and recognizing these problems can positively affect the people who live in fear, and is a step towards changing the mindset of the neighborhood. A state wide gang injunction will change and alter the quality of life as we know it to exist today, because it will give law enforcement the tools and resources they need to battle the gang problem. Conditions and provisions sanctioned have proven time and time again to eradicate the targeted gang from existence.

It is not illegal to be a gang member in the United States, but it is illegal to commit crimes in association with, at the direction of, or for the benefit of the gang, regardless if you are a validated gang member or not. It is further my opinion, if any state legislature and law maker studied the affects of a gang injunction within these cities, they would understand that gang members are not the only people who can be strong in numbers.

Anti-corruption laws
Information derived from the United states Attorneys' Bulletin May 2006; Marc Agnifilo AUSA; Kathleen Bliss AUSA; Bruce Riordan AUSA

Criminal street gangs number one source of profit is the sale and distribution of narcotics. These narcotics sales are coordinated through a hierarchical structure within the gang. This hierarchy can be linked to and range from the common gang member on the street, to the Mexican cartel responsible for bringing the drugs into the United States, and even the shot caller within a prison gang who claims and runs an area or neighborhood which the gang claims (referred to as a crew chief). The primary goal of an investigation is to dismantle the members who are considered leaders within the gang who run the sales and distribution of narcotics and guns. As the nation's new organized crime and the perpetrators of an ever-increasing percentage of the country's violent offenses, gangs have evolved to the point that federal law enforcement must pursue them aggressively.

There are several different approaches and statutes the Federal Government can use in battling this epidemic. What has been referred to as the "enterprise theory", federal statutes such as RICO (Racketeer Influenced and Corrupt Organization Act), Vicar (Violent Crimes In Aid of Racketeering) and the Drug Conspiracy/Continuing Criminal Enterprise (CCE).

In 1970, Congress passed the RICO ACT under 18 U.S.C. Sub-Section 1961-68. Properly used, RICO allows prosecutors to tell the entire story of a gang's existence in an indictment and later to a jury. Further, the prosecution can use every aspect of the gang and its history including, how it acquired its territory; how it makes and disposes of its money; how it uses coded language, hand signals, graffiti; and who it has killed and why, collaborated into one coherent story.

For a prosecutor to be able to show this "enterprise" and go forward with RICO/VICAR indictments on a gang member, the target gang must be defined as an enterprise under the racketeering statutes. The criminal group or gang must also have some structure for the making of decisions and a core of persons who function as a continuing unit. As long as the group indicted and being prosecuted exhibits the characteristics and continues to be legally defined as a criminal enterprise.

In state level prosecutions, to find a crime that falls under the definition of a gang crime utilizing the PC 186.22 section; gang enhancement, the prosecution must prove several defining characteristics to successfully utilize the gang enhancement. The gang member is from a validated criminal street gang, showing membership, territory, and a continual pattern of criminal activity. One method by the prosecution is to demonstrate the gang is a continual criminal enterprise with a propensity for continual criminal activity, which is known as a "predicate act".

Predicate, defined as,
1. Grammar and logic assert (something) about the subject of a sentence or an argument of proposition,
2. (Predicate on/upon) found or based on.

A predicate act
A previous act showing knowledge of or finding; basis of a current criminal act by means of showing a consistent pattern of criminal activity by a gang or gang member.

The prosecution must prove there is knowledge of this criminal activity within a certain gang and introduce past criminal behavior by gang members of the gang targeted. At least two previous criminal convictions of validated gang members of the targeted gang in which the prosecution is currently indicting. The previous convictions must contain three things.

1. The conviction has to be within three years of the present crime the District Attorney is currently prosecuting.
2. The previous convictions of the defendants of the predicate acts are gang members.
3. The current defendant has committed the crime for the benefit of, in association with or at the direction of the targeted gang.

A defendant has been arrested and charged by the district attorneys office for robbery. The prosecution, through circumstances and evidence brought forward by the investigator deems the crime committed by the defendant to be gang related. The prosecutor, during court proceedings, will then introduce two court certified copies of the previous convictions (within three years and at least two gang members from the same gang as the defendant). This is known as a "predicate act."

Having a broader understanding of the state level prosecution process in regards to a gang related crime and what has to be proven by the prosecution, will lead to a better understanding of the nexus to the federal level requirements. In relation to the RICO/VICAR statutes, the only significant difference between RICO and VICAR is the number of predicate acts required for successful prosecution. RICO requires two predicate acts that are related to each other and show a continuity of criminal activity. 18, U.S.C. sub-section 1962. VICAR requires the defendant to commit only one crime of violence as specified in 18, U.S.C. sub-section 1959, and to have committed this crime to maintain a position in the charged enterprise.

CCE or (Conspiracy and Continuing Criminal Enterprise), governs what the vast majority of gangs number one profit maker is; the sale and distribution of narcotics. This profit is not only gained from the sales and distribution of narcotics, but in some cases, gangs are directly involved in the taxation as well as the extortion of drug dealers within the neighborhood in which they distribute. Extortion not only in the traditional sense regarding the intimidation of businesses, but enslaving drug dealers who make minimal if any profit at all. This extortion can occur as the typical mafia mentality where the drug dealer is offered protection for a large cut of the profit and the taking at will any narcotic product for personal use and sales by the person committing the extortion.

Combating this at the federal level is difficult but can be proven if the members of the target gang are selling drugs in a coordinated fashion. With confirmation evidence from wire taps and other surveillance techniques drug conspiracy is a viable charging option for the federal prosecutor or (AUSA). Also added to this section, the prosecutor can charge a single conspiracy involving different subgroups committing acts in the furtherance of the conspiracy. Adding yet another tool to his tool box.

For example:

Not only the drug dealer being investigated who is selling a high volume of drugs, but persons who purchase drugs from them to re-sell at a street level can be charged with the same conspiracy or investigation as the target.

The CCE (Drug Conspiracy/Continuing criminal Enterprise) law offers is a twenty-year mandatory sentence for what is known as a "basic offense". In some cases at the federal level, depending on leadership, drug quantity, and income, because it is aimed at the principal administrators, organizers, or leaders of a narcotic trafficking enterprise,-the mandatory sentence is life in prison. Further with this statute, if a principle drug organizer or leader falls under the CCE violations and the prosecutor can prove the defendant is working under the furtherance of the CCE provisions commits an intentional killing, the defendant may be sentenced to death. A decision to seek the death penalty is determined by the prosecution who weighs the strength, evidence and other factors involved in the case.

In 2005, I was one of five investigators chosen to what ended up being the largest federal gang take-down in United States history. Known as "Operation Knockout". The investigation centered around a gang which showed a propensity for violence and murder, but also a drug distribution enterprise that reached from the United States to South America. Once the criminal enterprise was exposed, we were able to show a continuous pattern of criminal activity dating from the late 1950's. Over the years, this gang had developed an extreme hatred towards African Americans, law enforcement, as well as a neighboring rival gang. This hatred over the years was responsible for countless murders and drug trafficking that preyed on thousands of communities and funded the well known violent prison gang, "The Mexican Mafia". At the conclusion of this investigation, over 200 hundred gang members, affiliates and drug distributors were federally indicted under the RICO/VICAR Acts. Federal agents from the FBI, DEA, ATF and Immigration banded together with the Sheriff's Department and were extremely successful in dismantling one of the most deviant legacies in the history of gangs, utilizing the federal methods explained in this chapter.

First Steps for Society

It has taken a century to get where we are now and it will take decades to overcome and break the cycle. The pendulum can and will swing to the side of justice, and again raise the quality of life to a standard where society does not have to live in fear. If we take responsibility as a group and accept our failures it will be the first step towards what we all strive for, a peaceful and meaningful existence.

Our society has become pessimistic because of the constant social frustrations of gangs. If we stop living in fear and admit the gang's social acceptances and existence, collectively we break the cycle. Not a generational, geographical, or economical cycle but an entire list of factors which continues to fuel gangs and create a sense of social acceptance allowing it not only to survive, but to thrive.

Not too many people are aware of the resources a person has while incarcerated in state prison. These programs can keep the individual to a degree, in touch with society. Inmates have the ability to log on and surf the internet, though it is usually through illegal means, such as cell phones. There are fire walls and security agents which have been implemented so the inmate does not have the capability of running a criminal enterprise. Email is permitted on a limited basis, however it is screened through extremely rigid security procedures.

Some inmates manage to blog daily or weekly events, depending on access. Career criminals are natural manipulators and they WILL manipulate the system regardless of the safeguards and protections implemented. They know everything they send, print, author, and search for, will be monitored and reviewed. While reviewing one such web site I came across one of the most profound statements I have ever read or even heard from a gang member. This individual was serving a twenty five to life prison sentence. I was well aware of the prisoner's existence through prior investigations and knew why he was incarcerated.

He wrote of his life and the road he took to end up incarcerated. In most writings by inmates an attempt is made at justifying their creation as well as how and why they ended up in the "system." Excuses are often regurgitated by the inmate, but in the end the constant manipulation we have come to see so many times, jumps off the page. Not in this case though. Having been involved in so many investigations and having vast knowledge of the life of this person, I knew what he wrote was true.

There was no "beating around the bush" and nothing was embellished. He told the truth about his life. There were no excuses, no heartfelt stories and lies of abuse. The author never blamed society or generational family gang members which swallowed his life and created a monster. Even though he was addicted to heroin, he never mentioned that drugs had clouded his decisions by making him vulnerable to gang life. After all, there are plenty of people addicted to drugs who have never been affiliated with gang membership. He never once spoke of being forced or coerced into a life he did not want to lead. No, he told the truth. As I finished reading the blog, I noted that the last paragraph summarized and validated my years of research, interviews, and ultimately my opinion on why the subculture we have grown to accept exists. The following is the last paragraph:

[SIC] "We all have choices, some big and some small, but both just as important. Every choice we make leads to the next choices, every action leads to the next action, and both choice and action have consequences. The consequences of bad choices are a very high price to pay for freedom, loved ones, death and despaire. Ask yourself if you are willing to pay this price, as for me this price has been too much. Not a day goes by that I don't wish I could take it all back and live life over again and do things differently. This is my story: I hope you have listened and that your own story will have a better ending. Remember, every day we are given a chance to start life over and new, it's all up to you! We all have a choice, what will you make?"

WE ALL HAVE A CHOICE. *Gary Sloan*

Chapter sixteen

Hand signs and symbols differ from region to region. The hand signs below will give you an understanding of basic digital manipulation. This section will establish a foundation to further develop gang expertise. Notice the shapes of the alphabet loosely formed; many signs have more than one letter in each respective sign. To assist you in the identification of these signs and symbols, actual photographs will follow the illustrations.

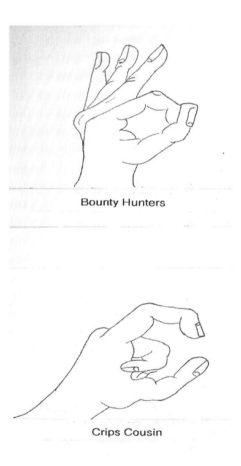

Bounty Hunters

Crips Cousin

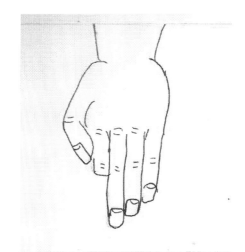

Piru Sign Blood

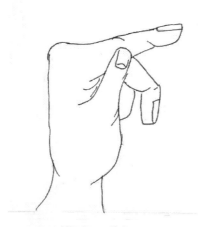

Kitchen Crip

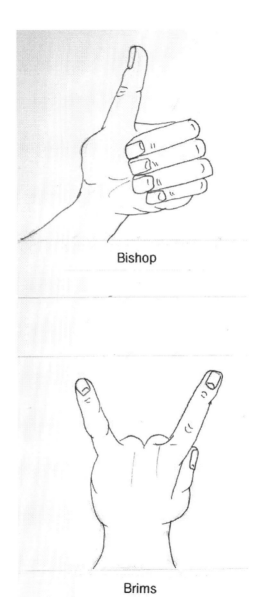

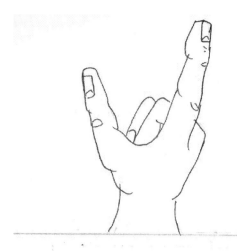

U Underground Crips

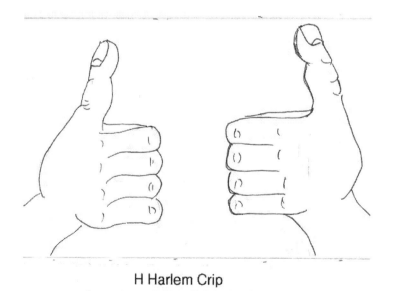

H Harlem Crip

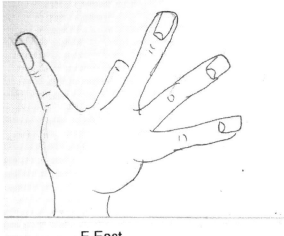

E East

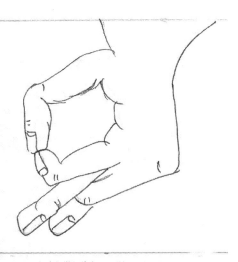

O Number Zero

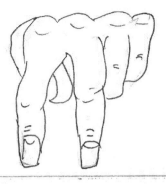

H Hoover Crip

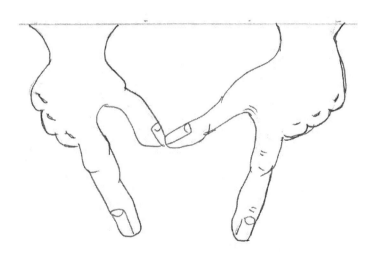

M Mafia Crip

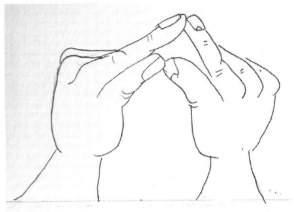
Athens Park Boys
(APBs)

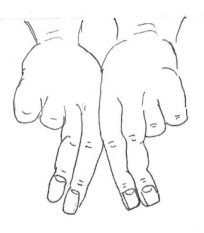
Mafia Crips

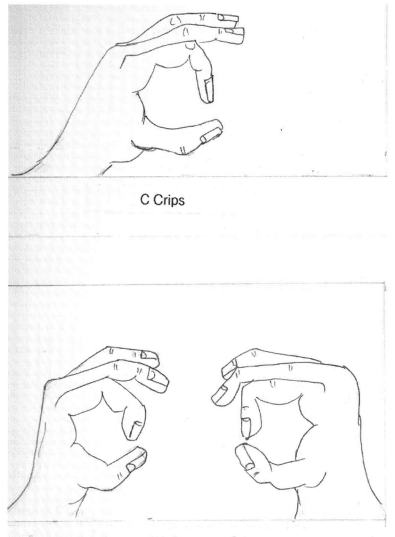

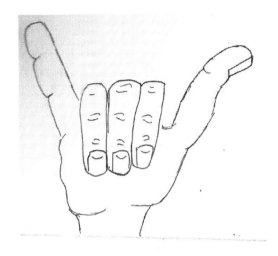

Primo

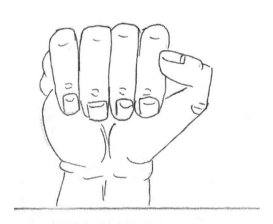

Power

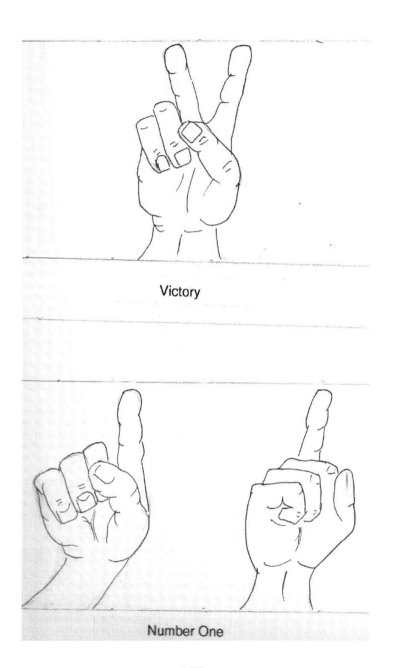

The following photographs are actual gang members demonstrating finger manipulation for the benefit of their gang. It is not important who and where they are from; this book will not participate in glorifying an individual gang member or gang. What is important is that you begin to notice the differences in angles and poses.

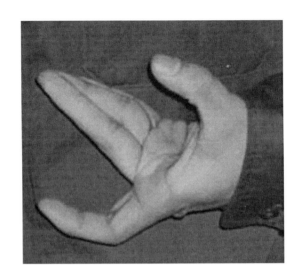

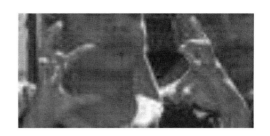

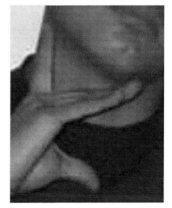

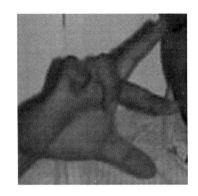

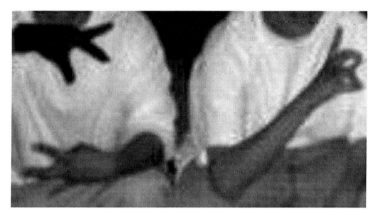

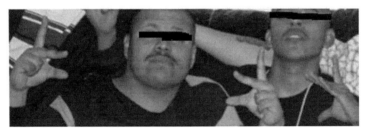

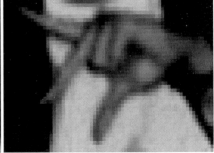

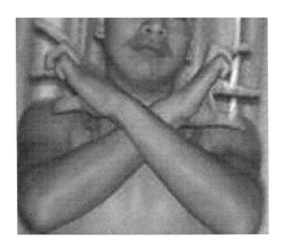

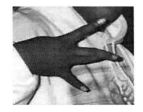

Chapter seventeen

Gang and Crime Scene Investigations

To be an effective gang investigator you have to devote your time and commit yourself entirely to this occupation. Upon making this commitment, the investigator must recognize one of the most important aspects to success is making yourself available 24/7. This means not only being available for normal work functions such as court, in-custody arrests and daily investigative assignments, but also available for the phone call off duty regarding gang related incidents; sometimes as simple as answering a question from a younger inexperienced patrol officer.

There is no room in gang investigations for a person who has the propensity for selfishness. Making yourself readily available both on and off duty will be the key factor to success. The second a gang investigator is called-out regarding a violent gang related crime, the investigator should already be thinking outside the box. Regardless of the incident or who is involved, every investigation should be treated equally and with the same tenacity. Whether it is a gang member who has been shot or an officer involved shooting, your emotions must be kept in check. Failing to maintain proper decorum can lead to a poor investigation and the appearance of a lack of professionalism. When emotions come between a detective and the investigation, key points can be missed and evidence and procedures lost and/or forgotten ultimately damaging your case during trial.

The investigator must think ahead, with the idea every case assigned will be going to a jury trial and no plea agreements will be made. To understand the importance of each aspect and prioritize what is relevant. The case should be viewed from a juror's perspective. Simplifying and categorizing the evidence to make the jury understand the power of the truth. Depending on the level of violence and circumstances surrounding an individual gang incident, each step and prioritization of key elements will differ. These elements will change with every investigation and are categorized as follows:

Crime scene and contamination
Officer and witness statements
Crime lab/CSI involvement
Suspects in custody or still outstanding
Department Of Children Services
Evidence collection
The authoring and service of search warrants
Suspect interviews or statements made prior to the arrival of the investigator
Officer safety hazards
The detention or availability of witnesses
Secondary crime scenes
Command posts and additional Law Enforcement resources
Shutting down geographical area's for the retrieval of evidence such as major streets or freeways
Gun sniffing dogs
Human sniffing dogs
Evidence dictating the incident as a gang crime

The investigators thought process must be that of a district attorney who will be presenting evidence to the jury. Also, the investigator must be thinking ahead as far as an appeal process if the suspect is found guilty. Understanding these key points, looking ahead and outside of the box during any investigation regardless of the circumstances, allows the investigator develop a mindset and understand the big picture.

The Evolution in technology and how we present cases to jury's have changed significantly. The large paper easel with fold over pages as if you were playing an old television game show has been replaced by a power point demonstration in opening and closing statements. This is an excellent tool because people in general are trained better through visualization as apposed to instructional type lecture. The Deputy District Attorney will walk the jury step-by-step through the entire case, what the crime scene looked like, the evidence located and the people directly involved in the case. Utilizing photographs taken by the investigator or crime lab technician, can give a firsthand visual account as to what really happened.

The investigator is coordinating the investigation; supervisors have the formal authority to make and/or override any decision the investigator makes, but will almost always defer. With the exception of exigent circumstances the investigator must have a clear understanding that time is on their side. Taking the few extra minutes to conduct an intelligence gathering interview, utilize resources, and show the same tenacity and professionalism towards every case will be the difference between conviction or acquittal. When a defense attorney can not prove or raise reasonable doubt to the innocence of their client, there is only one avenue left to afford their client a zealous defense; attack the credibility of the detective and the investigation they have conducted. The defense attorney will read every line and tear apart every detail of every report, look at all aspects of discovery evidence presented by the district attorney and attack any piece of evidence that has been overlooked or deemed of no evidentiary value. Jury's do not want to hear how tired an investigator was at the time of the incident, budget concerns, lack of resources or any excuse as to why it isn't a perfect investigation. Do everything possible to prevent the question, "Tell me detective; what else did you forget to do?" The defense will desensitize the jury to a point that the suspect's guilt or innocence becomes secondary to the work product of an inexperienced or lazy investigator.

It is the responsibility of the detective to close these gaps within their investigation and minimize any concern that can possibly be brought forth by the defense. The case lies solely on the shoulders of the detective so it is essential to know what is of evidentiary value and strengthen what will obviously be attacked. This is where the prioritization becomes so important and effective. If you as the investigator have identified the weakness within an investigation, then you must strengthen this aspect and make it a priority. Close the gaps of reasonable doubt by visualizing your case on trial; remember a large percentage of jurors only knowledge of the law and law enforcement procedure will be based on television and movies.

The next few pages are the time line, procedures, and utilization of resources from an actual investigation. This 30 hour period will give the reader a better understanding of the tasks and thought process of a gang detective.

Notification
2:30 AM: I received a telephone call at home from a supervisor. He told me patrol officers had been shot at by three gang members during a pursuit on the freeway. During the pursuit the gang members in the vehicle utilized their cellular phones and contacted several other fellow gang members in an attempt to avoid capture. The gangster's vehicle was involved in a collision into a guard rail terminating the pursuit. No weapons had been located inside the car and the vehicle was impounded as evidence. One of the suspects was transported to the hospital with a head injury. Gang members and family members of the suspects responded to the traffic collision and at the hospital. Several hostile gang members arrived at the hospital at the same time as the ambulance and attempted to free (lynch) him from custody. During this confrontation a gang member tossed a hand gun into his car as he was confronted by law enforcement.

Considerations:
Multiple crime scenes
Multiple suspects arrested
Unaccounted bullets fired by suspects
Unaccounted weapon recovery
Crime Lab call outs

Possible gun dog needed
Independent witness statements
Search warrants to all three suspects houses looking for more guns or ammunition

Arrival at the scene
3:15 AM: I drove to the first crime scene where the shots were fired and spoke to the officers involved. Their statements indicated the suspects had not fired at the officers. The suspects were possibly in the area of a rival gang with the purpose of finding a rival gang member and killing him. Two rounds were fired from the car as the officers watched from approximately twenty five feet away. The suspects fired their weapons in a random manner and never noticed the officers in their car next to them. The officers stated at no time did they ever see anything being thrown out of the car during the pursuit. Not knowing where the rounds ended up we conducted an article search to obtain the expended rounds by walking a line in the direction the weapons were pointed. Approximately 75 yards away, I saw a parked vehicle which had a hole in the windshield. The crime lab sent a team to photograph the area, extract the bullet from inside the car, and figure the trajectory of the bullets fired from the car. Further, I shut down the street where the incident occurred and requested a gun-sniffing dog to search due to sun light issues. I walked the streets and knocked on doors, apologizing for the early morning intrusion, but with an understanding this has to be done. Neutral parties are the best witnesses to corroborate an incident and are a must in any high profile or violent gang case.

Details
4:15 AM: The gun dog and his handler arrived and searched from the point of incident to the first major street. No weapon was located. During the search, members of the crime lab arrived. I briefed the crime lab technicians and asked them for distances measured from the area of incident to the parked vehicle, photographs depicting the area where the suspect vehicle was last seen as well as where the officers were parked,

photographs of the parked vehicle as well as the extraction of the bullet(s) found in the car.

A systems check showed the owner of the car lived at the house next to the parked car. The gun dog handler was advised to stay at the crime scene in case a second search was to be conducted. The officers involved explained their route of travel to me from the beginning of the pursuit to the end. Day light was now showing and I presumed the weapons had been thrown out of the window of the suspects car and onto the freeway and because of darkness the officers had not seen this occur.

Closing freeway
5:45 AM: I contacted the California Highway Patrol and requested their assistance in shutting down a one-mile portion of the freeway. I contacted the local sheriff station and utilized five deputies in a skirmish line along with the gun sniffing dog and his handler, to walk the distance of the shut down freeway and search for the weapons. No weapons were located and the search was terminated. Crime lab technicians concluded their search, located the bullets inside the front portion of the vehicles upholstery and extracted them for evidence.

Second crime scene
7:30 AM: I arrived at the second crime scene with crime lab technicians and they photographed skid marks and the damage caused by the traffic accident. I conducted an evidence search for weapons even though deputies had done a thorough search. A police officer should never allow their ego to get into the way of what is best for an investigation and if the investigating officer asks for a second search, then that is what needs to be done. Remember, the investigator is in charge of the entire crime scene and will ultimately be the one testifying in front of twelve people. No weapons were found and the search was concluded.

Interviews
8:00 AM: I arrived at the Sheriff Station to conduct interviews on all three suspects. Two of the suspects admit to me their role and the reason for being in the area. The suspects admitted to watching as the driver fired the hand gun. One suspect stated he was not aware of where the weapons were thrown because he was turned away from the driver, watching the police officers pursue them. All of the suspects admitted they never observed the officers next to them because they were focused the opposite direction. One thing that I was drawn to in each of the statements was that none of them were able to explain how the weapons were discarded. Even to the point of not having a clear answer as to whether they saw or heard a window being rolled down in an attempt to throw the weapons out of the car during the pursuit.

Search warrant
11:15 AM: I authored a search warrant to be served within the next 48 hours by the gang investigative team to all three suspects' residences. The search consists of looking for gang paraphernalia and additional weapons used by the gang members. Gang paraphernalia is crucial in utilizing gang enhancement laws which could add a substantial amount of time if the suspects are found guilty. I spoke with the deputies involved in the pursuit and arrest of the suspects to ascertain if any additional supplemental reports were needed. During the incident at the hospital, one person was arrested and two were identified as being involved in the assault on deputies and attempted lynching of the wounded suspect.

Still no weapon
2:15 PM: Twelve hours into the investigation and I still don't have the weapon(s). Remember, identify what is important to the case. You want to close the gap of reasonable doubt to the twelve people who will decide the fate of the suspects. Minimize what you have already established and concentrate on what you cannot yet substantiate. What can be proven at this point? My knowledge of the suspects and their gang status, the reason why they were in a gang rival area, the time of night the incident occurred,

my knowledge of the deputies experience who searched for the weapon inside the vehicle, and the expended casings located inside of the parked vehicle. But where did the guns go?

Going home
4:30 PM: All the suspects have been booked and interviewed. It will be a few days before any reports from the lab are finished regarding the possible caliber of the weapon(s) used as well as the photographs being developed. In my mind, I have covered every avenue regarding the solicitation of statements made by the officers, witnesses and suspects. A thorough search has been made and search warrants have been authored. Now because the suspects are all accounted for and arrested time is on my side. At times you should stand back for a different perspective on any aspect of an investigation. This perspective can come from a fellow partner or friend, even a family member, however, the bottom line is there will be a time in every investigation in which you must stop and go home. Tired minds lead to substandard investigations and I can admit on this day, I was getting tired. I left the station and drove home never letting go of the question; "where were the guns discarded"?

Delegation
5:00 PM: During this investigation I concentrated on what needed to be proven. Delegation of assignments is extremely important because you just can't expect to do everything as an investigator. I had never actually gone to the tow yard to inspect the vehicle or what was left of it. Numerous people had searched the car and searched it well; even removing door panels and the dash board. There did not appear to be anything left to search. I continuously played statements made by the suspects in my mind. How is it they could be so truthful on some questions, even to the point of incriminating themselves regarding the discharge of the weapon, but unable to give any explanation to the whereabouts of the guns.

Follow up
5:00 AM, the next day: I drove to the tow yard to snap additional photos of the suspect vehicle. Due to curiosity, I examined the car and began searching it for any evidence that was overlooked. I learned years ago that when searching a vehicle it is best to stand by the open drivers side door and simply look for a few minutes. I noted something strange about the floor. The passenger side floor was actually raised higher then the drivers side by at least four to five inches. I walked over to the passenger side of the vehicle and looked down at what appeared to be a stitched in floor matt which is not uncommon in older cars. I pushed down on the floor matt and noted the metal was soft and creased easily. It was obvious what I had stumbled on, an illegal compartment commonly referred to as a "clavo". I contacted the handler for the gun sniffing dog as well as a detective from our Narcotics Bureau who specialized in utilizing a narcotic sniffing dog.

Canine alerts
7:30 AM: Both handlers arrived and one by one, I had them search the interior of the car with their respective dogs. Both dogs alerted on what appeared to be a hidden compartment which gave cause for a search warrant. I drove back to my office and wrote a quick warrant for the search of the car and had it signed by a judge. Both dog handlers stayed with the vehicle to preserve the chain of evidence and eliminate any fabricated defense theory.

Jackpot
10:00 AM: After returning to the tow yard with the signed search warrant, I utilized a pick to open up the hidden compartment. These compartments are manufactured to be opened in several different ways. Most of the time, there is going to be a mechanism or simple toggle switch that activates the compartment to open. Or as elaborate as activating buttons from a radio in a combined sequence that only the owner is aware of. The compartment contained what I had so desperately looked for a little over twenty four hours earlier; not only the hand gun used in the shooting, but

also a semi-automatic assault weapon. Even though the narcotic sniffing drug dog had alerted on the compartment no drugs were recovered. However, a strong odor of methamphetamine emitted from the area the guns were found, indicating the compartment was recently used for the storage of a large amount of drugs. The guns were recovered and transported to the crime lab to be test fired and also swabbed for DNA. Some times, we get lucky.

Detective Gary Sloan

Glossary

Acceptance- Approval
Affiliation- Forming an alliance with a gang.
Afoot- Just about to happen
Aryan Brotherhood- A white street gang.
Banging on- Flashing signs to another gang member
Bitch- Derogatory comment referring to women or a subservient male.
Bloods- A black street gang.
Burn out line- Fraudulently purchased cell phone.
Carnal- Brother
Cherry patch- Location where crime is abundant
Colors- Gangs identify themselves by wearing specific colors.
Consensual encounter- Free to leave.
Crack baby- infant born to an addicted mother.
Crippin- Robbing or stealing.
Crips- A black street gang
Detention- Not free to leave.
Down- Placing the gang above all else.
Early morning wake up call- Detectives serving search warrants.
Flashing- Hand gesture symbolizing the gang.
Gang signs- Hand signals used to identify the gang.
Gangsta rap- Music glamorizing the gangster lifestyle.
Hard candy list- Marked for death/ hit list
Hells Angels- A white biker gang
Heroin- Opiate based illegal drug.
Hit up- Demanding an individual to claim their gang.
Hyna- Girlfriend of gang member
Holding the keys- Controls situations.
Homies- Short for home boy; friends or fellow gang members.
Hood rat- Female living within the gang lifestyle.
Hook up- a relationship with a female for the purpose of manipulation.
Injunction- Court order.
In the hat- Marked for death.

Jumped in – A ritual utilized while initiating a new gang member. Established gangsters beat up the volunteer until he has paid the price to join them.
Junta- Meeting.
La Causa- The cause.
Llavero- Individual who holds the key.
Methamphetamine- Manufactured stimulant.
Mexican Mafia- Known as la Eme they control most of the Hispanic gangs throughout the Southern California prison systems.
Missions- Orders to be carried out.
Neighborhood- Territory belonging to the gang.
Paraphernalia (drug)- A device or instrument used to ingest narcotics.
Parole- Supervision of individual released from prison.
Probable cause- A legal reason to stop an individual.
Probation- Supervision of individuals sentenced to less than one year.
Prospect- prospective gang member.
Recognition- An important aspect of the gang lifestyle.
Rite of passage- Showing loyalty through a ritual utilized by gangs.
Ruse- deflection to law enforcement.
Secretaries- Females used as facilitators of communication for incarcerated gang members.
Sexed up- Females are initiated into the gang through sex acts.
Shot caller- Decision maker from the gang.
Slang- Verbiage used on the street.
Status- Level achieved within the gang.
Strawberry- Female crack addict selling her body for sex.
Vagos- A white biker gang.
Walked/Grandfathered in- The gang member has grown up in the neighborhood.

The following pages are actual forms used by detectives, police, probation, and parole officers.

CITY OF _____ POLICE DEPARTMENT
PROOF OF PERSONAL SERVICE OF DETERMINATION AND FIELD INTERVIEW REPORT FORM

I am employed in the county of ___. I am over the age of 18 years and not a party to the within entitled action. My business address is ____
CA. 92702

On _____, 2009, _____ a.m./p.m. I served a true copy of the Notice of Determination by personally delivering a true copy thereof to the person whose name and address is indicated on this form.

▶ **GANG AFFILIATION:** _____ ◀

Last name: _____ First name: _____ M/N: _____

D.O.B.: __/__/__ Moniker: _____ AKA: _____

CHECK APPROPRIATE BOXES

SEX: ☐ MALE ☐ FEMALE HEIGHT | FEET: ___ INCHES: ___ WEIGHT: ___

HAIR: ☐ BLACK ☐ BROWN ☐ BLONDE ☐ RED ☐ GRAY ☐ OTHER: ___

EYES: ☐ BROWN ☐ HAZEL ☐ BLUE ☐ GREEN ☐ OTHER: ___

RACE: ☐ AMERICAN INDIAN ☐ ASIAN ☐ BLACK ☐ HISPANIC ☐ MULTIPLE
☐ PACIFIC ISLANDER ☐ WHITE

NATIONALITY: ☐ USA ☐ OTHER: ___

COMPLEXION: ☐ ACNE|POCK ☐ DARK ☐ FRECKLED ☐ LIGHT|FAIR ☐ MEDIUM ☐ PALE ☐ SALLOW

HAIR TYPE: ☐ SHAVED ☐ BUTCH ☐ COMEBED BACK ☐ CURLY ☐ FLATTOP ☐ MILITARY
☐ BALD ☐ STRAIGHT ☐ THICK ☐ WAVY
☐ OTHER: ___

HAIR LENGTH: ☐ COLLAR ☐ LONG ☐ SHORT ☐ SHOULDER

FACIAL HAIR: ☐ BEARD ☐ CLEAN SHAVEN ☐ FU MANCHU ☐ FUZZ ☐ GOATEE
☐ LOWER LIP ☐ MUSTACHE ☐ SIDEBURNS ☐ UNSHAVEN
☐ OTHER: ___

TEETH: ☐ STRAIGHT ☐ CROOKED ☐ MISSING ☐ GAP ☐ STAINED ☐ BUCK ☐ BRACES
☐ OTHER: ___

CLOTHING WORN: _____

ADDRESS: _____ CITY: _____

PHONE: HOME ( ) _____ WORK ( ) _____ CELLULAR ( ) _____

DL/OR ID#: _____ SSN#: _____ CASE|CITE#: _____

CII #: _____ OTHER MISCELLANEOUS ID #: _____

▶ **LOCATION OF SERVICE:** _____ ◀
▶ **REASON FOR CONTACT:** _____ ◀

▼ **STATEMENT! – CONDUCT! – INDICIA SHOWING AFFILIATION!** ▼

_____
_____
_____
_____

☐ REGISTRATION REQUIREMENT PER CPC § 186.30
☐ ENTERED INTO CAL-GANGS

- POLICE DEPARTMENT GANG INVESTIGATION DE

CITY OF _____ POLICE DEPARTMENT
NOTICE OF DETERMINATION

IN RE: THE MATTER OF _____ GANG

NOTICE OF DETERMINATION THAT _____ GANG IS A CRIMINAL STREET GANG WITHIN THE MEANING OF CALIFORNIA PENAL CODE § 186.22.

TO: THE PERSONS AFFILIATED WITH THE _____ GANG AND

_____. DATE: _____, 2009
(NAME OF PERSON BEING SERVED)

YOU ARE HEREBY NOTIFIED that the above mentioned is a criminal street gang engaging in a pattern of criminal street gang activity within the meaning of California Penal Code § 186.22(e).

"Pattern of criminal gang activity" means the commission of, attempted commission of, conspiracy to commit, or solicitation of, sustained juvenile petition for, or conviction of two or more of the following offenses, provided at least one of these offenses occurred after the effective date of this chapter and the last of those offenses occurred within three years after a prior offense, and the offenses were committed on separate occasions, or by two or more persons:

1) Assault with a deadly weapon or by means of force likely to produce great bodily injury, 2) Robbery, 3) Unlawful homicide or manslaughter, 4) The sale, possession for sale, transportation, manufacture, offer for sale, or offer to manufacture controlled substances, 5) Shooting at an inhabited dwelling or occupied motor vehicle, 6) Discharging or permitting the discharge of a firearm from a motor vehicle, 7) Arson, 8) The intimidation of witnesses and victims, 9) Grand theft, as defined in subdivisions (a) or (c) of Section 487, 10) Grand theft of any firearm, vehicle, trailer, or vessel, 11) Burglary, 12) Rape, 13) Looting, 14) Money Laundering, 15) Kidnapping, 16) Mayhem, 17) Aggravated mayhem, 18) Torture, 19) Felony extortion, 20) Felony Vandalism, 21) Carjacking, 22) The sale, delivery, or transfer of a firearm, 23) Possession of a pistol, revolver, or other firearm capable of being concealed upon the person in violation of paragraph (1) of subdivision (a) of Section 12101, 24) Threats to commit crimes resulting in death or great bodily injury, as defined in Section 422, 25) Theft and unlawful taking or driving of a vehicle, as defined in Section 10851 of the Vehicle Code, 26) Felony theft of an access card or account information, as defined in Section 484e, 27) Counterfeiting, designing, using, attempting to use an access card, as defined in Section 484f, 28) Felony fraudulent use of an access card or account information, as defined in Section 484g, 29) Unlawful use of personal identifying information to obtain credit, goods, services, or medical information, as defined in Section 530.5, 30) Wrongfully obtaining Department of Motor Vehicles documentation, as defined in Section 529.7, 31) Prohibited possession of a firearm in violation of Section 12021, 32) Carrying a concealed firearm in violation of Section 12025, and 33) Carrying a loaded firearm in violation of Section 12031.

YOU ARE, FOR THIS REASON, FURTHER NOTIFIED THAT ACTIVE PARTICIPATION IN A CRIMINAL STREET GANG COULD SUBJECT YOU TO PROSECUTION UNDER THIS LAW! CALIFORNIA PENAL CODE § 186.22

_____
Chief of Police

POLICE DEPARTMENT GANG INVESTIGATION DETAIL
1/2009

DEPARTMENTO DE POLICÍA DE LA CIUDAD DE
AVISO DE DETERMINACIÓN

AVISO DE DETERMINACIÓN QUE LA PANDILLA LLAMADA _____PANDILLA ES UNA PANDILLA CALLEJERA CRIMINAL BAJO DE LA DEFINICION DEL CÓDIGO PENAL DE CALIFORNIA § 186.22.

A: LAS PERSONAS AFILIADAS CON LA PANDILLA _____ Y A

_____. FECHA: _____, 2009.
(NAME OF PERSON BEING SERVED)

POR LA PRESENTE ES USTED NOTIFICADO que las susodicha organización es una pandilla callejera criminal envuelta en un repetición de actividad criminal callejera bajo la definición del Código Penal de California § 186.22(e).

"Repetición de actividad criminal de pandilla" significa el cometido de, el atento cometido de, conspiración de cometer, o solicitación de, petición juvenil sostenida para, o convicción de dos o más de las siguientes ofensas, siempre y cuando como mínimo una de estas ofensas ocurrió después de la fecha efectiva de este capitulo y la ultima de esas ofensas ocurrió dentro tres anos después de una ofensa previa, y las ofensas fueron cometidas en ocasiones separadas, o por dos o r tres personas:

1) Asalto con arma mortal o por medios de fuerza que puedan producir gran daño físico, 2) Robo, 3) Homicidio o homicidio involuntario, 4) La venta, posesión para la venta, transportación, fabricación, oferta para vender, o oferta para fabricar substancias controladas, 5) Disparar a una vivienda habitada o a un vehículo de motor ocupado, 6) Disparar o permitir a otro disparar un arma de fuego desde un vehículo de motor, 7) Incendio provocado, 8) La intimidación de testigos y victimas, 9) Robo mayor, como es definido en las subdivisiones (a) o (c) de la sección 487, 10) Robo mayor de cualquier arma de fuego, vehículo, carro de remolque, o embarcación 11) Robo con escalamiento, 12) Violación sexual, 13) Saqueo, 14) Lavado de dinero, 15) Secuestro, 16) Mutilación criminal, 17) Mutilación criminal agravado, 18) Tortura, 19) Extorsión mayor, 20) Vandalismo mayor, 21) Robo de auto a mano armada, 22) La Venta, distribución, o traslado de una arma de fuego, 23) Posesión de una pistola, revolver, o otra arma de fuego capaz de ser escondida en la persona en violación del párrafo (1) de la subdivisión (a) de la sección 12101, Código Penal de California, 24) Amenazas para cometer crímenes que resultan en muerte o gran daño físico, como es definido en las secciones del Código Penal 422, 25) Robo y apropiación ilegal o conducción de un vehículo, como es definido en la sección 10851 del Código de Vehículos, 26) Mayor robo de una tarjeta de acceso o información de cuenta, como definido en la sección 484e, 27) Falsificando, diseñando, usando, atentando de usar una tarjeta de acceso, como definido en la sección 484f, 28) Mayor fraudulento uso de una tarjeta de acceso o información de cuenta, como definido en la sección 484g, 29) Uso ilegal de información identificador personal para obtener crédito, artículos, servicios, o información medical, como definido en la sección 530.5 30) Obtener ilegalmente documentación del Departamento de Motores y Vehículos, como definido en la sección 529.7, 31) Prohibido poseer un arma de fuego en violación de la sección 12021, 32) Llevar un arma de fuego oculta es violación de la sección 12025, y 33) Llevar un arma de fuego cargada es violación de la sección 12031.

¡POR ESTA RAZÓN, ES USTED ADICIONALMENTE NOTIFICADO QUE PARTICIPACIÓN EN UNA PANDILLA CRIMINAL CALLEJERA LO HARIA SUJETO A SER ACUSADO BAJO ESTA LEY! 186.22 CÓDIGO PENAL DE CALIFORNIA.

Jefe de Policía

CITY OF   DEPARTMENT GANG INVESTIGATION DETAIL

▶ LAST NAME: _____ FIRST NAME: _____ ◀

☐ PROBATION ☐ PAROLE PROBATION/PAROLE NUMBER [_____] ☐ INFORMAL PROBATION

NAME OF PROBATION/PAROLE AGENT: _____

SCARS | MARKS | TATTOOS | ODDITIES (SMTO) – LIST GANG SPECIFIC TATTOOS FIRST
☐ NO SCARS/MARKS/TATTOOS/ODDITIES OBSERVED – SKIP THIS SECTION

S|M|T|O	SIDE BACK| FRONT| LEFT |RIGHT	LOCATION INNER | LOWER | OUTER | UPPER	PART OF BODY	DESCRIPTION OF S|M|T|O

AFFILIATE INFORMATION

GANG AFFILIATION	LAST NAME	FIRST NAME	MI	DATE OF BIRTH
1				
2				

AFFILIATES' ADDRESS (CITY, STATE, & ZIP CODE)	(AREA CODE) TELEPHONE NUMBER
1	
2	

VEHICLE INFORMATION IF APPLICABLE

☐ DRIVER ☐ R/F PASSENGER ☐ L/R PASSENGER ☐ R/R PASSENGER ☐ OTHER: _____

YEAR	MAKE	MODEL	STYLE	COLOR	LICENSE	STATE

☐ PARENT(S)/GUARDIAN INFORMED SON/DAUGHTER IS AFFILIATING WITH A CRIMINAL STREET GANG

Attach color photograph here!
While not mandatory, if you are unable to take a photograph
Get a thumb print!
2' – 3' DISTANCE

LIGHT COLOR BACKGROUND

UPPER CHEST – FACE
IF WEARING GLASSES – TAKE ONE WITH AND ONE WITHOUT THE GLASSES

DO NOT WRITE ON THE FRONT OF THE PHOTOGRAPH

(LEGIBLY) **PRINT NAME AND ID NUMBER**

(LEGIBLY) **SIGNATURE**

I DECLARE UNDER THE PENALTY OF PERJURY UNDER THE LAWS OF THE STATE OF CALIFORNIA, THAT THE FORGOING IS TRUE AND CORRECT.

Executed on _____ _____, 2009 at
  f served in another city –
indicate: _____

RIGHT THUMB PRINT

INSTRUCTIONS:
1. Original to Probation Files
2. Copy to Parents
3. Copy to Minor

TERMS AND CONDITIONS OF PROBATION

During the period of your probation, you are responsible to your probation officer, who is a representative of the Juvenile Court. You are ordered by the Juvenile Court to obey these terms and conditions of probation:

Minor's
Initials

_____ 1. You are to report to your probation officer in person as directed. Transportation problems or poor weather conditions are not acceptable reasons for not reporting. You are hereby directed to report in person every _____.

_____ 2. You are to comply with all directions of your probation officer. You are to obey the reasonable and proper directions of your parents or guardian. You are not to spend the night away from home without **prior** parental permission.

_____ 3. You are to obey all laws, including traffic rules and regulations. You are not to operate a motor vehicle on any street or highway until properly licensed and insured. You are to report to your probation officer any arrests or law violations immediately.

_____ 4. You are to obey the curfew law of the city or county in which you live or any special curfew imposed by the Court, the probation officer or your parents/guardian; specifically: _____.

_____ 5. You are not to leave the State of California or change your residence without first getting permission from your probation officer. Prior to change of residence, you are to notify your probation officer of the new address. You are not to live with anyone except your parents or approved guardian without specific permission of your probation officer.

_____ 6. You are to attend school every day, every class, as prescribed by law, and obey all school regulations. Suspension from school and/or truancies/tardiness could result in action being taken by the Probation Department. You are to notify your probation officer by 10:00 a.m. on any school day that you are absent from school. If you are home from school because of illness or suspension, you are not to leave your home that day or night except to keep a doctor's appointment.

_____ 7. You are not to use or possess any intoxicants, alcohol, narcotics, other controlled substances, related paraphernalia, poisons, or illegal drugs; including marijuana. You are not to be with anyone who is using or possessing any illegal intoxicants, narcotics or drugs. Do not inhale or attempt to inhale or consume any substance of any type or nature, such as paint, glue, plant material or any aerosol product. You are not to inject anything into your body unless directed to do so by a medical doctor.

_____ 8. You are not to go any places of business disapproved by your probation officer, guardian or parents; specifically: _____

_____ 9. Your associates are to be approved by your probation officer and your parents/guardian. You are not to associate with any individuals whom you have met while in any of the County institutions. You are not to associate with the following individual (s): _____.

_____ 10. You are not to have any weapons of any description, including firearms, nunchucks or martial arts weaponry, and knives of any kind, in your possession while you are on probation, or involve self in activities in which weapons are used, i.e. hunting, target shooting.

_____ 11. You are to attend counseling as directed by your probation officer. You are directed to _____.

_____ 12. You are to enroll in and attend a vocational training program such as Regional Occupation Program (ROP). Compliance with their rules and regulations is viewed as part of your school responsibilities. You are to attend this program until further direction from your probation officer.

_____ 13. You are to seek and maintain employment on a (full or part-time) basis. You are to be employed on or before _____. You are to notify your probation officer immediately upon termination of employment.

_____ 14. You are: to pay restitution, fine, restitution fund, restitution fine in the amount of _____, beginning _____, and you are to pay at a rate of _____ per _____, to be paid on the _____ of each month.

_____ 15. You are to submit to search and seizure of your person and property at anytime by any peace officer without benefit of a search warrant.

_____ 16. You are to submit to a chemical test of blood, breath or urine as directed by the probation officer or any other peace officer.

_____ 17. You are to complete _____ hours of community volunteer work as directed by the probation officer.

_____ 18. You are to remain in placement as directed by the probation officer and you are to comply with the rules and regulations of that placement.

_____ 19. Your driver's licence has been (suspended/restricted to driving to and from school, work, and to seek employment) for _____

_____ 20. You are hereby ordered to obey the following additional terms of your probation.

(a) _____

(b) _____

(c) _____

JUVENILE
GANG TERMS AND CONDITIONS OF PROBATION

NAME _____

J _____

During the period of your probation, you are responsible to your probation officer, who is a representative of the Juvenile Court. You are ordered by the Juvenile Court to obey these terms and conditions of probation.

Minor's Initials:

_____ 1. You are to report to your probation officer in person as directed. Transportation problems or poor weather conditions are not acceptable reasons for not reporting.

_____ 2. You are to comply with all the directions of your probation officer. You are to obey the reasonable and proper directions of your parents or guardian. You are not to spend the night away from home without DPO permission.

_____ 3. You are to obey all laws, including traffic rules and regulations. You are not to operate a motor vehicle on any street or highway until properly licensed and insured. **You are to report to your probation officer any arrests, law violations or police contacts immediately**.

_____ 4. YOU ARE NOT TO BE OUT OF YOUR HOME BETWEEN **8 P.M. AND 5 A.M.** WITHOUT PRIOR APPROVAL OF YOUR PROBATION OFFICER.

_____ 5. You are not to leave the State of California or change your residence without prior permission from your probation officer. Prior to change of residence, you are to notify your probation officer of the new address. You are not to live with anyone except your parents or approved guardian without the specific permission of your probation officer.

_____ 6. You are to attend school every day, every class, as prescribed by law, and obey all school regulations. Suspension from school and/or truancies/tardiness could result in action being taken by the Probation Department. You are to notify your probation officer by 10 a.m. on any school day that you are absent from school. If you are home from school because of illness or suspension, you are not to leave your home that day or night except to keep a doctor's appointment.

_____ 7. You are not to use or possess any intoxicants, alcohol, narcotics, other controlled substances, related paraphernalia, poisons, or illegal drugs, including marijuana. You are not to be with anyone who is using or possessing any illegal intoxicants, narcotics or drugs. Do not inhale or attempt to inhale or consume any substance of any type or nature, such as paint, glue, plant material or any aerosol product. You are not to inject anything into your body unless directed to do so by a medical doctor.

_____ 8. You are not to be present in any know gang gathering area of the _____ gang as directed by your probation officer.

_____ 9. Your associates are to be approved by your probation officer and your parents/ guardian. You are not to associate with any individuals whom you have met while in any of the County institutions. You are not to associate with any member of the _____ gang or any other gang as directed by your probation officer.

_____ 10. You are not to possess weapons of any description, any weapon including but not limited to firearms, knives of any description, nunchucks, and martial arts weaponry. You are not to possess ammunition or weapon replicas. You are not to involve yourself in activities in which weapons are used including but not limited to hunting and target shooting. You are not to remain in any vehicle wherein anyone possesses a weapon, ammunition, or weapon replica.

_____ 11. You are to submit to search and seizure of your person, property, automobile, residence, or any container under your control at anytime with or without reasonable or probable cause by any peace officer or probation officer without benefit of a search warrant.

_____ 12. You are to submit to a chemical test of blood, breath or urine as directed by the probation officer or any other peace officer.

_____ 13. Do not remain in any vehicle either as a passenger or driver which you know or suspect to be stolen.

_____ 14. Do not possess nor remain in the presence of one who you know possesses any master key, lock picks, dentpuller, "slim jim," slide hammer, or other device you know to be an auto theft or burglary tool.

_____ 15. Do not appear at any Court proceeding unless you are a party, defendant in a criminal action, or subpoenaed as a witness.

_____ 16. Do not wear, display, use or possess any insignia, emblem, button, badge, cap, hat, scarf, bandana or any article of clothing which is evidence of affiliation with or membership in the _____ street gang.

_____ 17. You are not to be on any school campus where not enrolled without permission of the school administration.

_____ 18. Do not possess a beeper, pager, cellular phone or any other cordless or otherwise wireless communication device.

_____ 19. Do not possess graffiti of any form. Do not have in your possession or maintain paints, aerosol spray cans, pens, etching devices or other instruments usable in applying graffiti. Do not assist others in application of graffiti.

_____ 20. Carry valid picture identification at all times.

_____ 21. Do not obtain tattoos except as permitted by your probation officer.

_____ 22. Have no contact with _____

_____ 23. Report to the police agency for the area where you reside, as specifically designated by the Probation Department, within 72 hours of the imposition of this term of probation or your release from any custody imposed as part of this case disposition, whichever is later. Upon reporting, identify yourself to the police agency and submit a copy of the terms and conditions of your probation. Submit yourself to any photographing, fingerprinting or other identification procedure requested by the police agency.

_____ 24. **You are hereby ordered to obey the following additional term(s) of your probation:**

_____
_____
_____
_____
_____

I have personally read, initialed, and understand the Terms and Conditions of Probation that apply in my particular case as explained to me by the probation officer/ Defense Attorney. I understand that my failure to comply with the initialed items could result in my arrest and/or my return to court.

Date:_____   Signed: _____
                                         (Minor)

INSTRUCTIONS: _____
1. Original to Court – White   (Parent/Guardian)
2. Copy to Parents/Minor – Canary   _____
3. Copy to Probation File – Pink   (Attorney)
4. Copy to District Attorney – Gold   _____
                                         (Deputy Probation Officer)

DIVISION OF ADULT PAROLE OPERATIONS
SPECIAL CONDITIONS OF PAROLE (ATTACHMENT)

SUBSTANCE ABUSE/NARCOTICS RELATED	REASON	INITIAL
You will participate in anti-narcotic testing in accordance with instructions from the Division of Adult Parole Operations, your Supervising Parole Agent or any other agent of any law enforcement agency within the State of California.		
You will actively participate in a substance abuse treatment program as directed by the Division of Adult Parole Operations.		
You will enroll in and successfully complete a community based substance abuse treatment program or a County Prop 36 as directed by a Parole Agent or the BPH.		
You are not to be in, loiter near or travel past **high narcotic areas as defined in Health and Safety Code Section 11532**. These are areas where drugs are bought/used/sold. You will not associate with persons you know or reasonably should have known to be drug users/dealers.		
You are not to possess or have access to any personal communication devices without prior Parole Agent approval. (This includes but is not limited to a pager, cellular phone, two-way radio, etc.) You are not to possess or have access to any type of radio scanner capable of receiving any type of law enforcement radio communications.		
You are not to possess tools of the narcotic trade. (This includes but is not limited to gram scales, glass cookware, beakers, heating mantles, tubing, chemicals, solvents, cutting agents, packaging materials, manufacturing instructions, pay-owe sheets, police scanners or any other paraphernalia used in the manufacture/sale of narcotics)		
You are not to possess or have access to Acetone, Caffeine, Camping Fuel, Charcoal Lighter Fluid, Denatured Alcohol, Dimethylsulfone, Methylsulfonylmethane (MSM), Ephedrine, Ether, Freon, Hydriodic Acid (HI), Hydrochloric Acid (HCl), Muriatic Acid, Hydrogen Chloride Gas (HCl Gas), Hydrogen Peroxide, Hypophosphorus Acid, Iodide Salts, Iodine, Isopropyl Alcohol (Rubbing Alcohol), Methanol, Naphtha, Niacinamide, Nicotinamide, Vitamin B, Phenylpropanolamine, Red/White Phosphorus, Compounds containing Phosphorus, Psuedoephedrine, Sodium Chloride, Sodium Hydroxide, Lye, Caustic Soda, Sodium Thiosulfate, Sulfuric Acid or any other chemical used in the manufacture/production of illegal narcotics.		
You are not to possess or have access to medication (prescription or otherwise) whose primary ingredients are ephedrine or Psuedoephedrine.		
You are not to possess or have access to any books, magazines, printed material/notes/drawings, clothing or advertising of any kind detailing individuals, characters, words/phrases promoting the drug culture and/or the sales/use/production of any type of drug or controlled substance.		

DOE, JOHN GONZALES
PAROLEE NAME (Print/Type)

1

DIVISION OF ADULT PAROLE OPERATIONS
SPECIAL CONDITIONS OF PAROLE (ATTACHMENT)

ALCOHOL RELATED:		
You will totally abstain from the consumption of any alcoholic beverages or liquors.		
You are not to possess or have access to any type of alcoholic beverages or liquors.		
You will not be in, or in close proximity to businesses whose primary function is to sell or serve alcoholic beverages without prior approval from the Division of Adult Parole Operations. (This includes but is not limited to bars, clubs, gambling establishments/casinos, adult entertainment venues, etc.) If you are unclear whether or not a specific location is prohibited, you must first seek approval of the Division of Adult Parole Operations prior to entry into the establishment.		
GENERAL:		
You will report any and any/all law enforcement contact (whether routine or not) with any law enforcement officer, agency or agent to your supervising parole agent in person or via telephone within twenty-four (24) hours of the contact. When contacted by law enforcement, you must clearly identify yourself as an active parolee and by the name under which you are supervised by the California Department of Corrections & Rehabilitation.		
You are not to associate with your crime partner(s) from your commitment offense or any previous offenses. Specifically, you will not contact, or cause to be contacted, any party involved in any prior criminal offense, specifically _____ in any manner (in person, by telephone, by mail or through a third party) without prior approval of your Supervising Parole Agent.		
You are not to possess, or have access to law enforcement identification, insignia, badges, uniforms or other items identified with law enforcement without prior approval from your Supervising Parole Agent or the Division of Adult Parole Operations.		
You may not operate a motor vehicle without prior parole agent approval. You must provide a valid driver's license, current registration and valid vehicle insurance before approval may be granted.		
If you are deported and you re-enter the United States for any reason, you must report in person to the Santa Ana #1 Parole Unit located at 1600 North Main Street in the City of Santa Ana on the first business day following your return.		
GANG RELATED:		
You shall not engage in gang participation as defined in California Code of Regulations, Title 15, Section 2513(e).		
You are not to contact or associate with any gang member, active participant or associate of a gang. You will not contact or cause to be contacted any member or associate in any gang in person, by		

DOE, JOHN GONZALES
PAROLEE NAME (Print/Type)

DIVISION OF ADULT PAROLE OPERATIONS
SPECIAL CONDITIONS OF PAROLE (ATTACHMENT)

telephone, by mail or through a third party. **(No contact means exactly that.)**		
You will not wear, possess or display gang insignia or colors. You are not to possess, have access to and/or display any items or paraphernalia related to gang membership or association with any gang at any time. (This includes but is not limited to pictures, drawings, books, videos, magazines, clothing, banners, etc.) You will not correspond or keep correspondence from known gang members or associates. You will not apply tattoos of any kind to your person without prior approval from your Supervising Parole Agent or the Division of Adult Parole Operations.		
You will not loiter near or travel past areas where gangs congregate.		
FRAUD RELATED		
You are not to possess or have access to checks, credit/debit cards or any other financial instruments without prior approval from your Supervising Parole Agent or the Division of Adult Parole Operations.		
You are not to use any fictitious names or possess identification belonging to another person.		
You will not have access to a post office box or public storage facility without prior Division of Adult Parole Operations approval.		
MODUS OPERANDI		
You are not to possess or have access to any type of books, magazines and/or printed material, written notes/drawings of a subversive nature related to the overthrow of the government of the State of California or the United States of America.		
You are not to possess or have access to explosives, TNT, plastic explosives, chemicals, blasting caps, timers, wiring, housing or bomb making tools/material of any kind.		
You are not to possess or have access to any type of books, magazines, printed material and/or written notes/drawings detailing the manufacture/use, specifications, deployment or operation of any type of explosive material/device, anti-personnel device or "booby trap".		
You are not to possess or have access to burglary tools of any kind. You are not to carry or have on your person tools of any kind unless required by the course of employment and approved in advance by your Supervising Parole Agent.		
RESIDENCE		
You will maintain a residence with a street address or other dwelling as approved by the Division of Adult Parole Operations. You will conspicuously display the street, apartment, space or unit number on your residence for ease of identification by the Division of Adult Parole Operations. Ready and unobstructed access **(examples of obstruction include but are not limited to locked gates, animals such as dogs, vehicles, junk, etc.)** must be available to the		

DOE, JOHN GONZALES
PAROLEE NAME (Print/Type)

Probationer: _____

Date: _____

Deputy Probation Officer

DIVISION OF ADULT PAROLE OPERATIONS
SPECIAL CONDITIONS OF PAROLE (ATTACHMENT)

	and present it to law enforcement when requested.	
	It is your sole responsibility to comply with all of the laws registration requirements and provide proof of registration to the Division of Adult Parole Operations within twenty-four (24) hours of registration.	

Reasons For Special Conditions of Parole

Special conditions of parole can be imposed if there is a nexus or are reasonably related to the Subject's commitment offense, criminal conduct, and/or future criminality. A special condition of parole that bars lawful activity is valid only if the prohibited conduct either:
1. Has a relationship to the crime of which the offender was convicted.
2. Is reasonably related to defer future criminality
Conditions may regulate conduct that is not in itself criminal, but rather reasonably related to future criminality by regulating or prohibiting non-criminal conduct.

REASONS FOR SPECIAL CONDITIONS OF PAROLE

1	Subject has a history, supported by an arrest, conviction, or documented admission or pattern of illegal or illicit drug use.
2	Subject has a history, supported by an arrest, conviction, or documented admission or pattern of alcohol use and/or abuse, where continued use could result in criminal or harmful activity.
3	Based on factors and circumstances directly related to the Subject's commitment offense(s), the imposition of this condition will assist in the goal of preventing the Subject from committing subsequent criminal offenses under Federal, State, or local law enforcement. **These Factors include:**
4	Based on the nature of the commitment offense(s), a nexus exists between the behavior being displayed during the course of committing his or her prior crime(s), and the behavior that is being restricted by imposing this condition. **The nature of the commitment offense is described as:**
5	Based on previous offense(s) as noted in the subject's criminal history, the restrictions imposed by this condition will assist in the goal of preventing the Subject from committing subsequent criminal offenses under Federal, State, or Local Law. **Previous offenses include:**
6	Based on previous offense(s) as noted in the Subject's probation or parole violation history, the restrictions imposed by this condition will assist in the goal of preventing the Subject from committing subsequent criminal offenses under Federal, State, or local law, or additional violation of his or her conditional release. **Previous violations include:**
7	There is a documented history of psychiatric problems.
8	The subject's documented history reflects actions of predatory sexual behavior.
9	Based on behavior displayed by offenders convicted of similar crimes, or displaying similar criminal behavior, imposition of this condition may regulate conduct that is not in itself criminal, but rather reasonably related to future criminality.
10	Parole Outpatient Clinic referral as required per PC 3002.
11	Based on current federal, State, or local laws, or Regulations cited in the California Code of Regulations, Title 15, as described below, **this condition is imposed to ensure compliance with the following laws or regulations:**
12	Based on your lawful requirement to register as a sex offender pursuant to PC 290, and your designation as a High Risk Sex Offender, you are subject to relapse prevention treatment programs pursuant to PC 3008(b).

Parolee Signature   CDC Number   Date

DOE, JOHN GONZALES
PAROLEE NAME (Print/Type)

PLEASE ATTACH 3 COPIES OF CRIME/ARREST REPORTS (4 IF REQUESTING ARREST WARRANT).

APPLICATION FOR PETITION

SEND TO PROBATION OFFICE

POLICE USE ONLY

REF. AGENCY _____ CASE NO. _____

MINOR'S LEGAL NAME _____ (last) _____ (first) _____ (middle) _____ AKA _____

MINOR'S ADDRESS _____ (number, street, apt.) _____ (city) _____ (state) _____ (zip) _____ PHONE ( ) _____

DOB _____ AGE _____ ETHNICITY _____ SEX _____ HAIR _____ EYES _____ HGT. _____ WGT. _____

PLACE OF BIRTH _____ LAST SCHOOL ATTENDED _____ CITY _____ GRADE _____

OFFENSE _____ LOCATION _____ DATE _____ TIME _____

PLACE OF ARREST/CUSTODY _____ DATE _____ TIME _____ OFFICER _____

FATHER _____ (name) _____ (address) _____ (home ph.) _____ (bus. ph.) _____

MOTHER _____ (name) _____ (address) _____ (home ph.) _____ (bus. ph.) _____

GUARDIAN / ATTY. _____ (name) _____ (address) _____ (home ph.) _____ (bus. ph.) _____

CUSTODY CASES ONLY: PERSON NOTIFIED OF MINOR'S DETENTION _____ NOTIFYING OFFICER _____
DELIVERED TO J.H. BY _____ DATE _____ TIME _____ ADMITTED BY _____
COMMENTS: (INCLUDE POSSIBLE CUSTODIAL PROBLEMS) _____

ADDITIONAL INFO. FOR PROBATION (PLEASE INCUDE GANG AFFILIATION) _____

AFFIDAVIT: I REQUEST COMMENCEMENT OF PROCEEDINGS IN JUVENILE COURT. I DECLARE UNDER PERJURY THAT THE ABOVE FACTS AND THOSE CONTAINED IN THE ATTACHED REPORTS ARE TRUE.

PRINTED NAME _____ PHONE _____ EXECUTED ON _____ (date) _____ AT _____ (city) _____, CA.
SIGNATURE _____ TITLE _____ AGENCY _____

INTAKE: **PROBATION USE ONLY**

J # _____ APP.REC'D DATE _____ TIME _____ NCI DL _____ CUST. DL FEL _____ MIS D. _____

☐ IN CUSTODY ☐ ON H.S.P. ☐ O/R DATE _____ TIME _____ TO WHOM _____ NO. APP'S ATTACH. _____
COMPANIONS   J/A #   P.O.   STATUS   COURT DATE

TO DA: DATE _____ TIME _____ INT. P.O. _____ PH. _____ ASS'D P.O. _____ PH. _____
RECOMMENDED ALLEG. _____ MINOR ADMITS TO _____
TYPE HEARING: ☐ DET. ☐ P/T ☐ TRIAL ☐ DISPO.   TYPE PET: 601 602   NEW SUB SUP   777WIC 778WIC
SEND NOTICE OF HEARING TO: ☐ PARENTS ☐ GUARDIAN ☐ ATTORNEY   ☐ REQUEST WARRANT (PROB/POLICE)
APP. PREVIOUSLY SENT TO DA : FILING DEADLINE _____ ALLEG. _____
PET. ALREADY PENDING: ALLEG. _____ TYPE OF HEARING _____ DATE OF HEARING _____
ADDITIONAL INFO. FOR DA (INCLUDE PRIOR RECORD INFO. OR ATTACH CJI/WARD CARD) _____

DISPOSITION: P.O. _____ DATE _____ SPO APPROVAL _____
☐ REFER TO DA   ☐ 654 WIC ADMIN./DIV./FIELD   ☐ DISMISS   ☐ OTHER _____
CONDITIONS OF 654 WIC / REASONS FOR DISMISSAL (INCLUDE SANCTIONS) _____

INSTRUCTIONS TO CLERICAL:	CLERICAL ROUTING	INITIAL	DATE
☐ SEND _____	RECORDS		
☐ REFER TO _____	STAT CLERK		
☐ OTHER _____	LOG CLERK		

INTAKE AND TRANSMITTAL SHEET-PROBATION FILE

JUVENILE DETENTION DISPOSITION REPORT
(Print or Type)

☐ Corrected Copy
Page ____ of ____

A. LAW ENFORCEMENT

Name (Last, First, Middle) *		DOB (mm-dd-yyyy) *	Age	CII #		
SSN	DL #	PIN			Sex	Race

Detention Date (mm-dd-yyyy) *	Detaining Agency *	Booking Agency		
Charge 1 (Section, Code) * I M F	Charge 2 (Section, Code) * I M F	FP Card/OCA # *	Booking/Cite #	Disposition Date (mm-dd-yyyy)
Charge 3 (Section, Code) * I M F	Charge 4 (Section, Code) * I M F	Crime Report #	Warrant # (Specify Charge #)	Disposition Code

B. PROBATION

Date (mm-dd-yyyy)	Disposition Code			
	Charge 1	Charge 2	Charge 3	Charge 4

☐ Detained ☐ Not Detained ☐ Fingerprinted ☐ Not Fingerprinted

C. PROSECUTION

Date (mm-dd-yyyy)	Disposition Code			
	Charge 1	Charge 2	Charge 3	Charge 4

D. JUVENILE COURT

Date Filed (mm-dd-yyyy)	Judicial District #	Petition #	Consolidated Petition #

Chrg	Charges & Enhancements at Time of Disposition Section & Code	Degree	File Level I M F	Final Plea Admit Nolo	Dismissal Code	Finding Sustained / Not Sustained / Not Guilty-Insane	Date (mm-dd-yyyy)	Disposition Level I M F 17 PC
1								
2								
3								
4								

Disposition (Sentencing) Date (mm-dd-yyyy)	☐ Firearms Prohibited	PROCEEDINGS SUSPENDED:	Date (mm-dd-yyyy)	Code

Chrg	Disposition Code	Probation Months	Confinement CYA Months / Juvenile Hall Days / Days Susp.	Other Programs (X)	Concurrent (X)	Consecutive (X)	Fine / Suspend (X)	Restitution (X)	Costs (X)
1									
2									
3									
4									

Remarks ☐ Court Ordered Booking

E. ADMONISHMENTS & WAIVERS

(Required for Sustained Judgement:)
☐ Minor waived counsel ☐ Minor represented by counsel

(Required for "Admit" or "Nolo" plea:)

Minor was advised of, and understood:	Yes	No	Minor was advised of, understood and waived:	Yes	No
• Charges and direct consequences of admission	☐	☐	• Privilege against compulsory self incrimination	☐	☐
Court found admission was knowledgeable, intelligently made and voluntary	☐	☐	• Right to confront and cross examine witnesses	☐	☐
Defense counsel concurred in minor's admission	☐	☐			

I certify that the foregoing is a correct abstract of the disposition of arrest and court action in this case. (Certification required for conviction)

Clerk of the Court (Print or Type) - Name (First, MI, Last)	Title	Date (mm-dd-yyyy)	County

JUS 8716 (Rev 06/2001)   Copies: DOJ - Purple   Arresting Agency - Blue   Court - Green

Note: Fields with an asterisk (*) in the Law Enforcement Section are mandatory